The Irish Setter

POPULAR DOGS' BREED SERIES

AFGHAN HOUND	*Charles Harrisson*
ALSATIAN (German Shepherd Dog)	*Jos. Schwabacher and Thelma Gray*
BASSET HOUND	*George Johnston*
BEAGLE	*Thelma Gray*
BOXER	*Elizabeth Somerfield*
CAIRN TERRIER	*J. W. H. Beynon, Alex Fisher and Peggy Wilson*
CAVALIER KING CHARLES SPANIEL	*Mary Forwood*
CHIHUAHUA	*Thelma Gray*
COCKER SPANIEL	*Veronica Lucas-Lucas*
COLLIE	*Margaret Osborne*
DACHSHUND	*E. Fitch Daglish, Amyas Biss and J. V. Crawford*
DALMATIAN	*Eleanor Frankling and Betty Clay*
DOBERMANN	*Fred Curnow and Jean Faulks*
FOX TERRIER	*Elsie Williams*
GOLDEN RETRIEVER	*Joan Tudor*
GREAT DANE	*Jean Lanning*
GREYHOUND	*H. Edwards Clarke and Charles Blanning*
IRISH SETTER	*Janice Roberts*
LABRADOR RETRIEVER	*Lorna, Countess Howe and Geoffrey Waring*
OLD ENGLISH SHEEPDOG	*Ann Davis*
POODLE	*Clara Bowring, Alida Monro and Shirley Walne*
PUG	*Susan Graham Weall*
SCOTTISH TERRIER	*Dorothy Caspersz and Elizabeth Meyer*
SHETLAND SHEEPDOG	*Margaret Osborne*
SHIH TZU	*Audrey Dadds*
SPRINGER SPANIEL	*Dorothy Morland Hooper and Ian B. Hampton*
STAFFORDSHIRE BULL TERRIER	*John F. Gordon*
WELSH CORGI	*Charles Lister-Kaye and Dickie Albin*
WEST HIGHLAND WHITE TERRIER	*D. Mary Dennis and Catherine Owen*
WHIPPET	*C. H. and Kay Douglas-Todd*
YORKSHIRE TERRIER	*Ethel and Vera Munday*

THE IRISH SETTER

JANICE ROBERTS

POPULAR DOGS
London Melbourne Sydney Auckland Johannesburg

Popular Dogs Publishing Co. Ltd

An imprint of the Hutchinson Publishing Group

17–21 Conway Street, London W1P 5HL

Hutchinson Group (Australia) Pty Ltd
30–32 Cremorne Street, Richmond South, Victoria 3121
PO Box 151, Broadway, New South Wales 2007

Hutchinson Group (NZ) Ltd
32–34 View Road, PO Box 40–086, Glenfield, Auckland 10

Hutchinson Group (SA) (Pty) Ltd
PO Box 337, Bergvlei 2012, South Africa

First published 1978
Second edition, revised, 1981

Printed in Great Britain by The Anchor Press Ltd
and bound by Wm Brendon & Son Ltd
both of Tiptree, Essex

British Library Cataloguing in Publication Data
Roberts, Janice
The Irish setter. – 2nd ed.
1. Irish setters
I. Title
636.7'52 SF429.17

ISBN 0 09 145510 3

To my loving dogs and understanding husband

ACKNOWLEDGEMENTS

My grateful thanks go to all those who have unselfishly given me their time, advice and encouragement in writing this book. It is impossible to name them all, but I am particularly grateful to the following:

Mr W. J. Rasbridge, the breed's foremost historian, for his valuable help and for greatly assisting with the bibliography and pedigrees; Mike and Sue Oakley for their photographs and drawings, for researching part of the history, and for compiling the list of champions; Mrs M. E. Stokes, Mrs W. E. Cucksey, Miss S. Lennox, and Mr and Mrs L. C. James for their reminiscences of pre- and post-war Irish setters; my veterinary surgeon, Mr David Green, B.Vet.Med., M.R.C.V.S., for advising on the ailments chapter; and Mr Raymond D. Long, B.Vet.Med., M.R.C.V.S.

I must also express my appreciation to those kind people overseas, some of whom I have never met, who have provided photographs and descriptions of the breed's progress in other countries: Mrs Norma Hamilton and Mrs L. Gledhill, Australia; the Southern Irish Setter Breeders, New Zealand; Mrs B. Simpson, South Africa; Mr and Mrs R. Martin Kenney, Canada; Mrs W. Duynkerke, Holland; and Mr P. Jacobs, Belgium.

My thanks are also due to the Kennel Club for the use of their library, and to both the Kennel Club and American Kennel Club for permission to reproduce their breed standards.

CONTENTS

ILLUSTRATIONS

Between pages 32 and 33

Between pages 64 and 65

IN THE TEXT

Figures 1 to 12 are by Susan Oakley

Author's Introductions

When Popular Dogs invited me to write this book I felt some natural reluctance in accepting. Certainly I have owned Irish Setters since 1958, but this is still a comparatively short time – and I considered that there were many people more experienced and better qualified than I to write about the breed.

However, the book which I was asked to write was a practical guide for the novice on how to choose a puppy and to bring the dog up to be a well-behaved, charming addition to the family, with further advice on how to cope with showing and breeding if the owner was bitten by the Irish Setter bug! These matters I did feel qualified to deal with, and with help from breed experts, friends and other sources of information I have also attempted a short chapter on the history of the breed.

It is my hope that this book will be useful to newcomers to the breed and helpful to novice breeders who should breed only with the true interests of the Irish Setter at heart.

1978

J.R.

As this second edition went to press, all lovers of the Irish Setter were delighted to hear that Mrs and Miss Tuite's Ch. Astley's Portia of Rua had been judged Supreme Champion at Cruft's 1981 – the first of the breed to gain this top award. This bitch had previously qualified to full champion in 1980.

There have been a few revisions for me to make to the second edition, and these are mainly in the History of the Breed chapter. Information on Progressive Retinal Atrophy (PRA) has been amended and also brought up-to-date in the light of recent developments. Parvovirus has been added to the chapter on ailments. My own satisfactory use of Vetbed in puppy-rearing has prompted an addition to the chapter on Breeding, and there have also been changes in the procedure of registering puppies. The appendices – the information section covering registrations, champions and breed clubs – have also been updated and there have been a couple of additions to the bibliography. Three of the photographs have been replaced.

1981 J.R.
Letchworth, Herts.

I

History of the Breed

The origin of the Irish Setter is lost in the obscurity of history. We know that, as early as the fifteenth and sixteenth centuries, dogs were described as 'setters' whose job was to locate game for falconing or netting: but this does not mean there was a specific breed. It is more likely that the term was used to refer to dogs – probably Spaniels – who were trained for this task.

There have been attempts to provide the Irish Setter with an ancestry going back to the beginning of the Christian era, but the results are not very convincing. Various breeds have been suggested as ancestors or contributors. Most authorities agree that the Spaniel played a large part – though which particular Spaniels, and where *they* came from is open to argument. Other breeds mentioned have included the Celtic Hound, the Pointer and the Bloodhound. Again, the evidence is weak.

What is certain is that a distinct type of dog, called a Setter, existed by the beginning of the eighteenth century; and that, not much later, there was a recognizable variant peculiar to Ireland.

This Irish Setter was bred by sporting gentlemen for their own use. A fascinating record of their preoccupations and interests is in the diary kept by Sir Francis Loftus, of Mount Loftus, Kilkenny. Here he describes his bitch, Quail:

> Mr Cooper made me a present of Quail in June, 1817. She was then three months old, of his own true blood (he breeds in and in). She was red-and-white, the red not very deep, about the middle size, extremely handsome, and as good a bitch as ever hunted, never committed a fault in her life – but was too slow in roading in the potato fields – was fast, stout, high-mettled, and extremely docile. She was the best rat-killer that could be, and fond of water.
>
> She was as good a brood bitch as ever was seen, often came to heat twice in one year, but never less than twice in three years. Generally had nine pups. She was an excellent nurse, but her puppies varied in size and colour, some being yellow-and-white, and some black-and-white. In general they were long and silky coated, long sterns and very much feathered. She gave one that was as smooth as a pointer. All those she gave, which were trained, were as good as I could have wished them to be.

Apart from this kind of record, Sir Francis gave day-to-day details of his dog training programme, interspersed with notes on feeding, exercise and so on.

Quail was red-and-white, and the basically white dog, with large red or chestnut markings seems to have been favoured by the Irish sportsmen. The self-coloured red, with occasional white markings seems to have emerged late in the eighteenth century and was, at first, the preserve of a few dedicated enthusiasts.

I suspect that this 'whole red' was bred then for much the same reason that it is today – for its beauty. Certainly, books on shooting contain many references to the difficulty of seeing the red dog under many sporting conditions compared with the white-and-red. In fact at one time, handlers of red dogs tied large white handkerchiefs round their necks to make them more visible. All this suggests that anyone breeding primarily for sport, who persisted with the red dog, had some motive other than efficiency.

However, the opposite view was put by Mrs Florence Nagle, a distinguished breeder of dual purpose Irish Setters in more recent years; that if it was hard for the handler to see the red dog, it was equally hard for the birds to see him. Another expert, T. G. Teasdale-Buckell, had a rather ambiguous attitude to the Irish Setter – and, indeed, to all things Irish: for instance '. . . the fact that the Irish Setter is the worst colour in the world to see in a Scotch mist can be well understood not to matter in Irish atmosphere and manners of thinking.' But even he had to admit, somewhat grudgingly, that he had got closer to birds with Irish Setters than he had ever managed to do with English Setters or Pointers. '. . . the birds behave differently, probably mistaking the Irish Setter for a Scotch fox . . . What they obviously did not expect was that there was a man behind.'

By the middle of the nineteenth century the type was well established, and the distinguished dog writer, 'Stonehenge' could go into some detail in comparing Setters and Pointers:

The peculiar characteristics of the English and Irish Setters, as displayed in the field, are great speed, activity, endurance, capability of bearing cold and wet, and of standing the rough work of the moors, in all of which good qualities the Irish Setter is even better than the English. He not only has these to perfection, but he also exaggerates the wilfulness and want of steadiness so remarkable in the setter as compared with the pointer, while at the same time, he is just as incapable of bearing the heat of the sun without water. Indeed, some rough coated setters . . . cannot work at all when their skins are dry and, unless they can run into a pool every half-hour at least, they blow like porpoises and are utterly useless.

'Stonehenge's description of the current type of Irish Setter is easily recognizable to a modern owner. The head was moderately heavy, less broad in muzzle, less square in profile than the Pointer. The eye was 'sparkling and full of spirit'. The ears were 'long and thin and covered with soft, silky hair, slightly waved'. The neck was long, thin and flexible. The back and loin appeared weaker than the Pointer's and the ribs

not so round and barrel-like . . . The hindquarters are not usually so muscular as that of the pointer, but the thighs being longer and the hocks usually stronger, the power is quite as great . . . The shoulder-blade is very long and fine . . . The true arm should be very long and the elbow is placed so low as to be fully an inch below the brisket . . . The hind legs and feet are clothed with hair, or 'feathered' as it is called, in the same way as the fore-legs, and the amount of this beautiful provision is taken into consideration in selecting a dog for his points . . . The colour of the Irish is generally a rich dark red, with still darker muzzle sometimes actually black, but more often a rich mahogany, the same dark shade running down the back to the stern, which has the short hair as dark as the muzzle. Many of them have more or less white about their limbs, . . . the less white they have, the more thorough-bred they are considered. The tail furnished with a fan-like brush of long hair . . . should never be carried over the back or raised above the level of its root.

The colouring of the breed obviously took time to stabilize. Earlier than 'Stonehenge', in 1845, Youatt wrote that 'The Irish sportsmen are a little too much prejudiced with regard to particular colours. Their dogs are either very red, or red and white, or lemon coloured, or white patched with deep chestnut.'

Youatt had some interesting information on current prices. Irish Setters were more expensive than their English equivalents or Pointers. 'Fifty guineas constituted no unusual price for a brace of them and even two hundred guineas have been given.' It is difficult to translate 1845 prices into a modern equivalent but we would certainly be talking about thousands rather than hundreds! Youatt doubted whether the Irish were as much better than their competitors as the prices suggested and 'whether, although stout and hard-working dogs and with excellent scent, they are not somewhat too headstrong and unruly.' (This latter trait crops up in writings on the breed from the early nineteenth century to the present day!)

Youatt also reported the setter's better qualities.

[A dog] ill with distemper, had been nursed by a lady more than three weeks. At length, he became so ill as to be placed in a bed, where he remained a couple of days in a dying state. After a short absence, the lady, re-entering the room, observed him to fix his eyes attentively on her and make an effort to crawl across the bed towards her. This he accomplished, evidently for the sole purpose of licking her hand, after which he immediately expired.

The devotion and eagerness to please of this dog will be familiar to many owners.

In 1859 the first dog show was held, for Setters and Pointers only; an indication that the breeds had now to some extent defined and their owners welcomed comparison and competition. The entries for early shows are interesting. In 1860 it was worthwhile to have a class for Irish Setters at the Birmingham show. At Dublin, in 1875, Irish Setters made sixty-six entries, of which twenty-three were red-and-white. A year later at Cork the figures were ninety-six entries, and thirty-six red-and-white dogs. The atmosphere of competition was increased by the introduction in 1865 of field trials in which the working abilities of dogs could be matched and compared.

Up to this point the Irish Setter had been almost wholly a working gun dog. But not long after showing became a recognized pastime a difference appeared between the worker and the show dog. The divergence is dramatically illustrated by the career of that great dog, Ch. Palmerston. He was bred, about 1862, by Mr Cecil Moore, who had a kennel of working gun dogs. Palmerston was not considered a good worker but was most successful as a show and stud dog. He was acquired by Mr T. Hilliard and began his show career. (There are stories that he was about to be put down as useless in the field but there seems no actual evidence of this.) Palmerston was soon a Champion and continued showing to a ripe old age. As a stud dog he had a profound impact on the breed. In 1936 Mr W. J. Rasbridge could refer to five direct male lines in Irish Setter pedigrees, one of which came from Palmerston. However, in the same article he pointed out that none of Palmerston's descendants were then active in field trialling.

The first attempt to codify the show points of the Irish Setter came with the formation of the Dublin Irish Red Setter Club in 1885, and the Club's production of a breed description and scale of points for judging a year later. Their description of the breed has, with relatively minor modifications, become the breed standard of today (see Chapter 6).

The working and show strains continued to flourish and mix during the last years of the nineteenth century and early years of the present century. However, several things contributed to lessen the demand for the Irish Setter as a working gun dog. 'Driving' grouse moors became popular – with rows of beaters driving the game towards the guns. This resulted in bigger bags for more guns, but made the slower, more skilful shooting with Setter or Pointer a rarer pursuit. Again, increasing mechanization of agriculture, at least in parts of England, changed shooting habits. Dog shows and field trials continued during the First World War almost uninterrupted until the end of 1916 – but the war and its subsequent social and economic upheavals contributed to the decline. Finally, the continuing 'troubles' in Ireland from 1916 onwards and the abandonment of many Irish estates undoubtedly struck the working Setter hard.

There has been a good deal of debate over the years about the quality of the Irish as a working dog – a debate neatly summed up by Major Harding Cox... 'Like a certain "little girl with a naughty curl, right in the centre of her forehead" it may be said of the Irish Setter "When it is good, it is very, *very* good, but when it is not, it is horrid!"'

Another good illustration of the Irish Setter having a mind of his own was given by G. T. Teasdale-Buckell, who had shot over and field trialled the famous Plunket. In his opinion, the finest Irish Setter he ever shot over was a son of Plunket's who

> had the peculiar luck of always finding birds when, by the manner of the other dogs, there appeared to be none about.

However, this dog would only work 'for real':

> ... out of the shooting season he was as useless as an ill-broken, careless puppy. He would run up birds without appearing to smell them before they rose, or to see them afterwards. Instead of waiting on your every wish, as he did in the shooting season, he took no interest whatever in the proceedings, and you could not cheat him into believing business was meant by the use of blank or any other cartridges.

Yet sportsmen persevered with this eccentric, wilful and often slightly mad breed, even when some had begun to think that the

Irish Setter had been overtaken in speed, endurance and accuracy by the English Setter and the Pointer. J. Wentworth Day gave an excellent description of their reasons, in a chapter significantly entitled The Wild Irishman

> . . . as a charming companion, a decoration, an occasional inspiration; as a light and lively element in the shooting landscape; as a racy addition to the humdrum world of everyday utility, I would have him every time. He is one of those people who add colour to life, grace to the scene, charm to everyday work and that rare, ineluctable quality of the light-hearted cavalier to otherwise serious matters.

In the period between the two world wars, there were still several kennels of working Irish Setters but as the period wore on, and especially in the 1930s, the Irish Setter became more a show and pet dog.

An indication of the Irish Setter's growing popularity in this period can be found in the registration statistics, issued annually by the Kennel Club. For instance, twice as many Irish Setters were registered in 1935 as had been in 1925. The annual total of registrations climbed steadily throughout the thirties and it is interesting to discover that in 1931, probably the worst year of the Depression in Britain, no fewer than 1464 Irish Setters were registered.

As has happened in the breed before and since, the story of the show dog in the inter-war period was one of a combination of domination by a few kennels and the success of a few, independent dogs. To list all the influential dogs of this period would need a separate volume. However, two or three of the more influential and successful pre-war kennels, and individual dogs can be briefly mentioned.

The show ring was dominated by the Rheolas and related stock right up to the Second World War. Mrs Ingle Bepler started breeding Irish Setters in 1894 and continued until 1941. She imported a dog from Holland, Ch. Clancarty Rhu of pure English bloodlines which was to have a great effect on her strain, especially when, mated to Ch. Carrig Maid, he sired Ch. Rheola Toby, who was a direct ancestor of Sh. Ch. Rheola Bryn.

Sh. Ch. Ypsilanti, one of the great bitches owned by Mrs Ingle Bepler, was sired by Clancarty Rhu. Another lovely bitch was Sh. Ch. Rheola Didona, considered by Mrs Ingle Bepler to be the best bitch she had bred. However, many contemporary experts have said that her greatest bitch was Didona's daughter, Ch. Norna, which was sold as a puppy to Mr P. H. Holme, who later became President of the ISAE. Norna was bought back by Mrs Ingle Bepler who then resold her to Mrs M. Ogden of the successful Borrowdales, where she had five of her six litters, which contained seven CC winners – a record which stood until 1979 when it was beaten by Sh. Ch. Cornevon Primrose. She also found time, between litters, to win eighteen CCs before her early demise at seven and a half years from torsion of the stomach. Mrs Ingle Bepler's Rheola Benedict had a great stud career, siring eleven CC winners.

A dog called Young Phil, which was born in 1900, has been described by Mr W. J. Rasbridge as being 'perhaps the greatest stud influence of the century'. His sire was Ch. Charleville Phil and his dam was Ch. Young Nora. He sired at least nine CC winners and his influence was such that he is to be found, many generations back, in most important modern pedigrees. Apparently, he wasn't as good-looking as his sisters, particularly Ch. Florizel, but his prowess as a sire of winning stock was most impressive.

Another dog who was very influential as a producer of both show and working stock was Gorse of Auburn, born 1917, by Galahad ex Auburn Nellie. His son, Ben d'Or, founded the famous Sulhamstead strain of field trial Irish Setters, and was also a CC winner himself.

J. A. Carbery, of the Boyne strain, was the most successful breeder of the twenties. His Ch. Barney of Boyne was the sire of both a field trial champion, Sulhamstead Token d'Or, and a full champion, Hundridge Mary of Boyne, among other winners. A bitch, Mrs E. Baker's Ch. Gadeland Neula of Boyne, had two litters of importance to the present day Irish: her first litter was to Sh. Ch. Rheola Bryn, and the other was to Bryn's son, Sh. Ch. Shamus of Ballyshannon, Miss Thorne-Baker's great show dog. The Boynes seem to have provided foundation stock for several kennels, such as the Whitwell's large Ardagh kennel and the James' Wendovers. Bessie of Gadeland was a daughter of Neula and she produced Ch. Wendover Biddy and Maureen of Wendover, who was the dam of Sh. Ch. Wendover Sugar, perhaps the best pre-war Wendover. The James bought another influential bitch from Mr Carbery – Wendover of Boyne. She produced

Wendover Rona, the dam of Wag of Wendover, who sired Sh. Ch. Raycroft Mediator.

Ch. Barney of Boyne also sired the Foots' Beorcham Blazes, and Ch. Terry of Boyne sired the foundation bitch of Miss Manuelle's Nutbrown kennel.

Mrs Whitwell's Ardagh kennel included the great bitch International Champion Delaware Kate, who won eleven CCs during 1927/28; she was a good worker and won at field trials. She won her title in England, Ireland, America and Canada, which is a record for the breed. Ch. Ravenhill Phil was another famous member of this kennel. He was the sire of seven CC winners and eight field trial winners. Ch. Jim O'Moy, born 1923, sired nine CC winners, including Mrs Ogden's Ch. Menaifron Pat O'Moy, who won twenty-two CCs, and thus shares with Ch. Hartsbourne Popsy, the breed record for the greatest number of challenge certificates won. He was also a field trial winner.

Another dog to sire nine CC winners was Ch. Crispian O'Kilner. He also won best in show at the Kennel Club show in 1928.

Mrs Eileen Walker's foundation bitch, Val, was born in 1926 from the successful mating of Sh. Ch. Rheola Bryn and Rheola Mallie. Val produced the first Hartsbourne champion, Hartsbourne Jade. From this kennel came Ch. Hartsbourne Vanity, a beautiful bitch who had a marvellous show career including best in show all breeds Glasgow Championship Show 1930, best bitch in show Kennel Club 1932 and best in show Cheltenham 1934. This was the beginning of a success story which was to continue until Mrs Walker's death in 1970.

Mrs F. Nagle's most successful Sulhamstead field trial strain were also good-looking dogs, capable of winning on the bench. Her Field Trial Champions, Sulhamstead Sheilin d'Or, S. Valla d'Or, and the famous dog, Sulhamstead Baffle d'Or, who won both the KC Derby and the Pointer and Setter champion stake, were all show bench winners.

Joe Braddon was successfully campaigning Moyra of Halcana, Nutbrown Sorrel and Ch. Wendover Biddy amongst others, during the thirties and he has since become a household word in dogs as a famous all-round judge.

During the 1930s an increasing number of Irish Setters were going blind for no obvious reason and breeders were baffled as to the cause. In those days 'hereditary defects' were unknown, as such; they have since become the veterinary surgeons' 'religion'. This blindness was known as 'night blindness' as Setters would blunder into obstacles at night. It was later named Progressive Retinal Atrophy.

Progressive Retinal Atrophy is a type of blindness which gradually worsens, ending in total blindness. The first symptoms (bumping into things) manifest themselves in twilight or at night, hence the misnomer 'night blindness'. The condition occurs in both eyes and is not painful. There is no form of treatment and therefore complete blindness is ultimately inevitable.

This eye disease is hereditary and is carried by a simple autosomal recessive gene. An animal can carry the gene without itself being actively afflicted – in fact, having normal vision – but if mated to a dog which also carries the recessive gene, the resultant litter will most probably contain a PRA case or cases, probably in a ratio of one in four.

A suspected carrier can be discovered – or cleared – by test-mating. This is done by mating a suspect to a blind Setter and rearing at least six puppies to an age when a correct diagnosis can be made. If there is even one case of blindness in the litter, then the suspect is a carrier. If there are none, the suspect is cleared of carrying the PRA gene.

Irish Setters are apparently the only breed in which the disease manifests itself at such an early age. From about twelve weeks old. an examination with an opthalmoscope by a qualified person can determine the presence or absence of the active disease of PRA This early diagnosis was a great help when it came to test-mating the breed in the late 1940s. However, the minimum age to which the whole litter must be kept for testing is now six months.

Test-mating is still the only method of checking the carrier potential of an Irish Setter and it is, even so, not 100 per cent reliable. In a litter of six, if all the pups are normal sighted, the chances of error are only one in sixty-four, so it is reasonable to accept such a chance. With each additional pup, the chances of error diminish.

However, this test has been known to fail. There is a case history of a bitch being test-mated and producing seven pups, all with normal vision. She was presumed clear. In her next litter she had six PRA puppies proving she was a carrier. By a freak of chance her test-mating had given the wrong answer.

There is also the 'human error' element as even an expert can make a mistake!

Test-mating saved the breed from destruction thirty years ago so it has certainly proved its worth.

No one knew anything about PRA in the thirties and the incidence of blindness was attributed to various causes other than hereditary. Unfortunately the most influential sire of the pre-war period was Rheola Benedict, who proved to be a carrier, as did many Rheolas. It was fashionable in those days for breeders to use the beautiful Rheola strain which produced such successful results in the show ring; thus PRA became widely distributed without breeders realizing what was happening.

However, Mr W. J. Rasbridge had his own suspicions of the possible cause of blindness. During the thirties he had undertaken breeding and pedigree research with the result that when, in 1945, there arose a cry of despair from breeders he was able to tell them what the trouble was and how to tackle the problem. Initially, this was met with considerable disbelief, and he had great difficulty in persuading some show ring breeders of the scientific validity of his approach. Mr Rasbridge asked the Kennel Club to take action against PRA and Mrs Nagle and Mrs D. M. Cucksey backed him up with separate requests.

In 1946, when Mr Rasbridge became secretary of the Irish Setter Association (England), the Association decided to act and enlisted the support of the Kennel Club. The KC tightened up registration requirements for Irish Setters by requiring a supporting declaration that neither the Irish Setter itself, nor either of its parents was a proven carrier of any hereditary disease of the eye, and altered the Show Regulations to bar any animal 'afflicted with a tendency to reproduce an hereditary disease'.

Leading breeders, who gave much-needed support to the actions of Mr Rasbridge in acquiring the above regulations, were Mrs D. M. Cucksey, Mr J. H. J. Braddon, Mrs E. F. Leighton-Boyce, Mrs Ogden, Mr and Mrs L. C. James and Mrs Darling.

Most of the recognized breeders turned to stock cleared by test-mating. However, a small minority continued with suspect setters. Also some pet owners bred litters, here and in Ireland, unaware of the PRA risk. Descendants of these suspect setters are still to be found. In this context they themselves are suspect, if coming from one or more proved carriers through a line not test-mated. Whether the gene has been transmitted remains uncertain.

Some beautiful and well-bred setters were discarded when test-mated and found to be carriers, including champions and CC winners. It was a heart-breaking business. Breeders used clear stud dogs and gradually, as the years passed, active cases of PRA became infrequent.

In this country nine matings have been revealed as producing cases of PRA since 1973, and others involving 'suspect' stock exported from here have been reported in the Antipodes. This established that the responsible gene still turns up in the breed occasionally. A few kennels have test-mated some stock.

The breed was rebuilt after the war based mainly on four PRA clear dogs. They were Branscombe Robyn, owned by Miss Samms, later Mrs A. J. Leighton Boyce; Mrs Jean Clarke's Brynmount Redgaynes Mars; Sh. Ch. Raycroft Mediator, owned by Miss Lamb, who later married to become Mrs Furness; and Mr and Mrs James' Beau of Wendover.

Branscombe Robyn and Brynmount Redgaynes Mars both sired four CC winners. Sh. Ch. Raycroft Mediator was the first male Irish Setter to win a CC after the war and was a great show dog. He sired eight CC winners. Beau of Wendover has had a tremendous influence on the breed through his son, Ch. Wendover Beggar.

As other dogs and bitches however were test-mated, the new basis of the breed broadened, including untest-mated imports from America and Ireland. Quite a few pre-war breeders and exhibitors retained an interest in the breed.

Mrs C. S. Darley, of the Watermill prefix, had her first Irish Setter as a schoolgirl in 1922 and was still breeding and exhibiting in the fifties. Some of her dogs are still to be found in the far reaches of present-day pedigrees. She was well-known as the writer of many interesting and informative articles and notes in *Our Dogs*.

Mrs 'Sulhamstead' Nagle kept her field trial flag flying from the twenties to the sixties with her tremendous string of FT champions. She gave up trialling when her great handler, George Abbott, retired in the mid-sixties. Mrs Nagle had eighteen FT champions, an amazing record. One very good-looking bitch was FT Ch. Sulhamstead Shielin d'Or.

Mr Jack Whittaker of the famous Gaelges started in the thirties but really made his mark after the war with Ch. Gaelge Copperplate of Ide, and his son, Ch. Gaelge Ardrew Pride, who won eighteen CCs and best in show Manchester, 1954. This was the start of a line which produced several generations of beautiful show champions, mainly bitches.

Miss V. Thorne-Baker exhibited her famous show champion Shamus of Ballyshannon before the war, and more recently campaigned Sh. Ch. Raycroft Chorus Girl to her title.

Mrs E. Scott-Gentles and Mrs D. Mateer have had an unofficial partnership from the 1930s to the present day. They have individually bred the occasional litter, and shown each other's breeding; the former's prefix being Portarlie and the latter's Loongana. Miss Moira Patterson bought a very good dog from Mrs Scott-Gentles, which she campaigned to become Sh. Ch. Roamer of Portarlie. Two more recent show champions bred by Mrs Mateer but owned by Mrs Scott-Gentles were Loongana Red Biddy of Portarlie and Loongana Lough Sheelin.

Mrs D. Cucksey, of Maydorwill fame, played an important part in the post-war reconstruction of the breed by using mainly clear stock: she successfully test-mated her Irish import Shandy of Maydorwill and also a bitch called Mischief of Maydorwill. She bred several show champions, including a dog which won his title in America. In the last litter she bred was one of her most successful bitches – Sh. Ch. Bodewell Beginagen, who won many CCs for her fortunate owners, Mr and Mrs J. Harper.

Mrs V. Page bought her first setter from Mrs Cucksey in 1950 – Maydorwill Meetosue. However, family commitments kept her from showing or breeding often until the middle sixties. Meetosue's great grand-daughter, Orichalc Freyja was a daughter of Brackenfield Dandelion, and Mrs Page successfully test-mated her clear of PRA in 1962. Freyja was then mated to Ch. Brackenfield Hartsbourne Bronze to produce Ch. Brackenfield Orichalc Juniper and Orichalc Juneberry, who was eventually mated to Sh. Ch. Cornevon Prince Charming to produce Sh. Ch. Orichalc Alchymist.

The Raycroft Irish Setters were founded in 1936 when Ray Furness was still Miss Lamb. She started with several good bitches, including Madonna and Mystery of Gadeland. During the war Mrs Furness bought the future show champion, Raycroft

Mediator; he was a most successful show dog and sire of several show champions, including Ch. Raycroft Rena who was best of breed and fourth in the best in show line-up at Crufts in 1951. She was the dam of four show champions. The present Raycroft stock goes back to Mediator on some lines. Mrs Furness has made-up sixteen champions herself and sold many more who became champions in other countries. Sh. Ch. Raycroft Hoobram Rich Corona won seventeen CCs and Sh. Ch. Raycroft Call Boy won eighteen CCs before they both went abroad.

It would be impossible in this short space to enumerate the many winners owned or bred by Mrs E. Walker of the famous Hartsbournes. It is enough to say that she bred twenty-eight CC winners, all except four since the war. She also won certificates with others not of her breeding.

Her outstanding pre-war winner, Ch. Hartsbourne Vanity, was mentioned earlier but another pre-war success was Vanity's grand-daughter, Ch. Hartsbourne Veracity.

In 1948 Mrs Walker imported Hartsbourne Senor of Shadowood from the USA, who had a big influence on the breed through his very beautiful daughter, Ch. Hartsbourne Popsy.

Popsy was a great bitch, winning twenty-two CCs under twenty-one different judges (the breed record for bitches). She also won best in show at Ayr in 1952. She produced six CC winners (all to Sh. Ch. Hartsbourne Tobias).

Tobias was by Hartsbourne Masterstroke ex Hartsbourne Flame, a bitch which Mrs Walker imported from Ireland. Flame had the 'shower of hail' markings which consisted of white dots scattered over her body coat – an extremely rare sight.

Tobias must rank as one of the top sires in the breed, having produced eleven CC winners, six of them in two litters from Popsy. One of the most important dogs from these matings was Sh. Ch. Hartsbourne Brilliant, who sired some beautiful stock before going abroad, including Ch. Brackenfield Hartsbourne Bronze, who was owned by Miss S. Lennox.

Another member of the Tobias/Popsy offspring was Sh. Ch. Hartsbourne O'Hara who carried on the Hartsbourne line, through his son, Sh. Ch. Hartsbourne O'Mara. When O'Mara was mated to Sh. Ch. Hartsbourne Honeysuckle, the result included the beautiful twins, Sh. Chs. Hartsbourne O'Kelly and Hartsbourne Tulip, also Sh. Ch. Hartsbourne Zinnia. So the saga went on; in 1966 Sh. Ch. Hartsbourne Starlight was born; she was a very beautiful bitch. Mrs Walker rated her one of her best.

Starlight was producing the last Hartsbourne litter bred by Mrs Walker when she died, while visiting America, in 1970; this litter contained the last Hartsbourne Sh. Ch., Carnbargus Hartsbourne Mattie. The majority of the dogs, along with the Hartsbourne affix, were left to Miss Lennox who still keeps the Hartsbourne name alive, along with her own Brackenfields.

Miss Sybil Lennox bought her first show dog in 1946, a bitch called Raycroft Meg who was by Sh. Ch. Raycroft Mediator. She was mated to Sh. Ch. Storm of Casamia, and produced a very good litter, which included a show champion and two more CC winners. There were two bitches in this litter which were very important to the Brackenfield strain: Brackenfield Pandora and Smallbridge Poppy.

Brackenfield Pandora was the dam of Sh. Ch. Brackenfield Primula, and her descendants carried down to Sh. Ch. Brackenfield May, a very successful show bitch, and Sh. Ch. Brackenfield Verbena.

Smallbridge Poppy was the dam of Ch. Brackenfield Poppy who when mated to Int. Sh. Ch. Erinhaven Dennis Muldoon (an American import) produced Brackenfield Dandelion, a potent stud-force. Unfortunately, Dennis Muldoon, who was imported by Eileen Walker, turned out to be a carrier of PRA; Miss Lennox test-mated Brackenfield Dandelion, and he was cleared of being a carrier, which was an enormous relief to the owners of his numerous descendants.

Ch. Brackenfield Hartsbourne Bronze was a great sire and he and Ch. Brackenfield Poppy also qualified in the field. He was the sire of many champions including Ch. Brackenfield Orichalc Juniper who maintained the stud pre-potency through successive generations of male champions. One of the most beautiful daughters of Bronze was Sh. Ch. Brackenfield Lozell Whisper.

The Hartsbourne/Brackenfield combination has proved a very sound basis on which many modern kennels have successfully built, including Mr Johnston's 'Allsquares', Mr Dodman's 'Barnsforde' kennel, Miss Albertis's 'Greenglades' and Mrs Gardner's 'Carnbargus' setters to name but a few. Mr and Mrs Cordwell's Ronnettas were based on Brackenfield Holly, who was the dam of Sh. Ch. Brackenfield Elm and Brackenfield Iris, foundation bitch of the Cornevons.

A very well-known present-day breeder, exhibitor and judge is Mrs M. E. Stokes of the Marrona affix, who owned and judged Irish Setters before 1930. She made a fresh start after the war with a presumably clear Wendover bitch, which she mated to Watendlath João O'Pandy to produce Marrona Milesian, her post-war foundation dog. Among other winners he sired Sh. Ch. Marrona Merope, who when mated to Sh. Ch. Norlan Paddy produced the very successful litter containing Sh. Ch. Marrona Marica and Sh. Ch. Marrona Marigold. Mrs Stokes's beautiful Sh. Ch. Marrona Meriel was best of breed at Cruft's in 1974.

As has been mentioned previously, W. J. Rasbridge did more to save the breed from ultimate destruction by PRA than any other person He did not breed many litters but the one containing the litter brother and sister, Watendlath João O'Pandy and Watendlath Jael O'Pandy was to have a lasting influence on the breed – Jael through her son, Sh. Ch. Watendlath Kevin O'Pandy, and João mainly through his two sons, Wendover Game and New Zealand Ch. Wendover Gary of Acres.

When Kevin was mated to a daughter of João, who also carried a line to another member of the João litter, he produced Brenhow Gay Gavin, who, in turn, was the sire of Mrs Brenda Howe's two Sh. Chs. Brendower Bounty and Brendower Bomber. However, Kevin's most important mating was to Sh. Ch. Wendover Roberta, who ranks with the all-time great brood bitches, having produced five CC winners. This litter contained Wendover Lola, who, when mated to Ch. Wendover Beggar, produced in one litter the two Sh. Chs. Wendover Katie and Wendover Kelly, and in another came Sh. Ch. Wendover Vagabond.

João was mated to Sh. Ch. Wendover Kelly to produce the litter brothers, Wendover Game, Gary, Glade and Australian Ch. Wendover Gleaner. Gary and Game have had an enormous influence on the breed, producing many famous champions and CC winners, some of whom have continued these winner-producing lines with their own descendants in the present-day scene.

This Watendlath/Wendover 'nick' is a large part of the post-war Wendover success story. I have previously mentioned, very briefly, the pre-war beginnings of the Wendovers, in the thirties, with mainly Boyne stock. Sh. Ch. Wendover Sugar was most successful; Wag of Wendover won a CC and then war broke out and stopped his career. He sired Sh. Ch. Raycroft Mediator, the first post-war CC winner. Mr and Mrs James bought Kerry of Wendover in 1939. With the outbreak of war the Wendover kennel was reduced and Kerry, with one ticket to his credit, went to Miss Kelly in Ireland. He was to prove influential in post-war history as the sire of Beau of Wendover, who came from Miss Kelly after the war, and in his turn sired Ch. Wendover Beggar, who has been one of the greatest sires in the breed and also won best in show at the West of England Ladies Kennel Society (WELKS) in 1955. His number of CC-winning offspring runs into the teens.

Beggar brings us back to the Watendlath/Wendover 'nick' with his matings to Wendover Lola. His daughter, Sh. Ch. Wendover Katie, was a great show bitch, who won many certificates and then went on to prove her worth as a brood bitch by producing a litter by New Zealand Ch. Gary of Acres (the only litter he sired before departing for New Zealand) which contained the two Sh. Chs. Wendover Gentleman and Wendover Nancy. They are numbered among the great Irish Setters of all time, and both had star-studded show careers, Gentleman retiring in a blaze of glory when he won best in show at Hove Championship Show. He has proved himself an exceptional sire, with a great many show champions and CC winners to his credit, including five in one litter. His most successful and influential son to date is Sh. Ch. Twoacres Troilus.

Katie's litter sister, Kelly, was an exquisite bitch, who made her mark on posterity with her litter by Watendlath João O'Pandy. Her son, Gary has already been discussed as the sire of Gentleman. However, her other influential son, Game, who was a dual CC winner, like his father, has a marvellous record as a sire.

He was bought, as a young adult, by Mrs M. Jarosz of the Joanma's affix. He was a worker himself and sired many show champions and field trial winners too, including Mr P. Heard's Ch. Joanma's Adriano, who won fifteen awards in field trials. Game's most influential son was Sh. Ch. Scotswood Barabbas, owned and bred by Mrs R. Bryden.

The third show champion in the Beggar/Lola litters was Wendover Vagabond, a great showman, who won best in show and reserve best in show at two championship shows in 1964 – quite an achievement. He was also the sire of many show champions and winners, including the James' present Sh. Ch. Wendover Racketeer.

The present-day Wendover kennels house many beautiful dogs, descended from predecessors described above. Mr and Mrs James have a wonderful breeding record and lovely and successful dogs, of which they must be justly proud. Their bloodlines have had great influence on the breed, both in this country and overseas, and they have started many newcomers on the road to success. Included among these is Mr and Mrs B. Rhodes' Fearnley kennel, which has been much influenced by the Wendover stud dogs. Also Mr and Mrs Norman of the Wellingham affix, who have been successful in campaigning Wendover Marauder and Wendover Lady May to their titles. Mr and Mrs Bob Heron started in Irish by making-up Sh. Ch. Wendover Caskey and their present stock descend from him. This includes Sh. Ch. Caskey's Zoe and Sh. Ch. Pollyanna of Caskeys.

Mrs M. Jarosz has owned Irish Setters since the mid-1940s. One of her most beautiful bitches was Wendover Yana, a dual CC winner from whom many of her present-day stock derive. I have already mentioned Wendover Game, her great stud-dog. Several show champions bear the Joanma's affix, including Sh. Ch. Joanma's Scampi who won the most CCs in the breed in 1976.

Mrs Jarosz has also owned and bred field trial winners. Joanma's Grouse won awards at field trials and also produced good workers, such as Joanma's Gull and Joanma's Pipit.

Mrs A. Mason (Acornbank) has kept Irish Setters for nearly forty years and has trained and used them for shooting, field trials and showing. She is a field trial and show judge and secretary of the Irish Setter Association, England, Field Trial Committee.

Mrs Rita Bryden bought her foundation bitch from Mr and Mrs James in 1961. She was Wendover Tritoma, who had a litter by Sh. Ch. Wendover Vagabond in 1963 which contained Scotswood Hot Sensation. This bitch is important as the dam of Sh. Ch. Scotswood Barabbas, one of the most prepotent sires in the breed. He was by Wendover Game.

Barabbas was a handsome dog with a beautiful head and expression, which his dam also possessed. It was a terrible blow to Mrs Bryden, and also to the breed, when he died at the early age of four. Even in this short time, he made an indelible impression on the breed; think what might have been, had he lived a normal life-span. He sired many champions and CC winners, even though he wasn't used extensively at stud. Two of his successful daughters are Sh. Ch. Marrona Meriel and Sh. Ch. Cornevon Primrose.

Mrs Bryden also kept Barabbas's litter sister, Scotswood Rachel, from whom her family continues. She also acquired a son of Barabbas, Margretwoods Caretaker of Scotswood, who seems to have inherited some of his sire's success as a stud dog, having produced seven CC winners. Mrs Neave bred Caretaker, retaining his litter brother, Sh. Ch. Margretwoods Craftsman.

Miss Judy Russell is another successful breeder/exhibitor who bought her foundation bitch from the Wendover kennels in 1956. She was very fortunate in obtaining a well-bred companion puppy who became Ch. Wendover Romance, winning five CCs and producing five CC winners, including three show champions, which places her among the great brood bitches. She was a wonderful bitch, as her last accomplishment shows, told in Miss Russell's own words:

> Perhaps her final glory was still to come when she undoubtedly wrote her name into the pages of history by gaining her qualifying certificate at the Yorkshire Gundogs Field Trials to become a full champion at the advanced age of 11 years and 3 weeks, after only three and a half weeks of very inept training, consisting mainly of 'sits' and 'stays' but including an invaluable session on the moors with the late Walter Edmonson of Crookrise pointer fame, who was impressed enough to encourage me to enter for the trials at which she ran a very good qualifier, impressing several notable field trial experts in doing so. It was a great relief that she chose the night before to catch a pheasant by the tail feathers as it got tangled in some sheep netting. Her willingness to learn and her obvious enjoyment of her new role were quite incredible. She knew far more from instinct than I could ever learn.

Romance was a very well bred bitch, being by Watendlath João O'Pandy ex Sh. Ch. Wendover Roberta (who also produced five CC winners). Her name is to be found in many of today's pedigrees of top-class dogs. One of her most important sons, by Sh. Ch. Wendover Vagabond, was Sh. Ch. Wendover Ballymoss, who sired the four show champions, Wendover Royalist, Wendover Lady May and Wendover Jeeves, and Twoacres Wayward Caesar.

Another Vagabond/Romance show champion was Timadon Ballywestow Festoon. Owned by Mr and Mrs G. Coupe, Festoon

Ch. Hartsbourne Popsy (22 CCs)

Sh. Ch. Raycroft Call Boy (*Anne Roslin-Williams*)

Sh. Ch. Wendover
Vagabond

Ch. Wendover Romance

)PPOSITE

Vendover Game
C. M. Cooke)

Aarrona Milesian
B. Thurse)

Sh. Ch. Watendlath Kevin O'Pandy (*Eldon Studios*)

Sh. Ch. Wendover Caskey

gained her sixteen points in Southern Ireland for her Irish title. Unfortunately, the Irish KC doesn't have our show champion title for gundogs so unless a dog qualifies in the field, they aren't recognized as champions. Festoon won best in show at the Irish Gundog Championship Show in Dublin. The Coupes' Wendover-based kennel has also produced Sh. Ch. Wendover Herald of Cuprea, who went to Canada with his owner, Mr Fanning; and their own Sh. Ch. Timadon Kendel.

Mrs June Coates founded her Twoacres kennel with Musbury Melisande of Twoacres, bought from her breeder, Mr D. Skuse. This bitch, who was line-bred to Sh. Ch. Brackenfield Hartsbourne Bronze, proved herself a great brood bitch, producing many winners, but her main claim to fame was with the famous 'T' litter. In January, 1968, she whelped what was to provide the breed record number of winners in one litter: the sire was Sh. Ch. Wendover Gentleman, one of the breed's greatest stud dogs.

The 'T' litter contained four show champions – Twoacres Troilus, Tamburlaine, Traviata and Teresa; the dual CC winner, Triton, who was unlucky not to get his title, and Tosca, a stud-book entrant.

The show champions were all enthusiastic showers. The two bitches, Traviata and Teresa, won seven CCs and six CCs respectively, plus many reserve CCs. Tamburlaine won best in show all breeds at Windsor in 1970. However, Troilus was by far the most successful show-dog, winning twenty-one CCs and fifteen reserve CCs, three groups, a championship best in show, and Irish Setter of 1971. His prowess as a sire is equally great, being Stud Dog of the Year in 1974, 1975 and 1976. He has sired five British show champions and several CC winners, plus several overseas champions.

One breeder who used Troilus successfully was Mrs Barbara Birch who mated her Sh. Ch. Morningstar Melanie to him twice, each litter producing a show champion – Moyna Mr O'Hara, owned by Mr G. Perry, and the multiple CC winning Moyna Michelle, owned by Mrs Sue Stobo. Mrs Birch also gave a home to an unwanted adult bitch, sired by Scotswood Barabbas, whom she subsequently campaigned to her title – Rickerscot Bridget Maguire.

As for my own dogs, the Cornevons were founded in 1958 when I bought a Maydorwill-bred dog, Cornevon Coppernob, as a companion. 'He's beautiful, show him,' said friends. So I did and was bitten by the bug. My foundation bitch, Brackenfield Iris, came into my hands as an unwanted two-year-old. When mated together, these two produced various winners, the two most important being Sh. Ch. Cornevon Snowstorm and Cornevon Snowbunting. The latter was a great brood bitch, producing four show champions in two litters; the first, by Wendover Game, contained Sh. Chs. Cornevon Prince Charming and Cornevon Cinderella, and the second, by Scotswood Barabbas, contained Sh. Chs. Cornevon Primrose and Violet. These Setters were the nucleus of my stock, all the above named having produced show champions themselves. The greatest of them all is Sh. Ch. Primrose who won seventeen CCs under seventeen different judges, and was Irish Setter of 1970 and 1972. She is also a prepotent brood bitch and won the title of Brood Bitch of the Year in 1974, 1975, and 1976. In her first litter to her half-brother Prince Charming, she produced the Sh. Chs. Cornevon Love Story, owned by Mr and Mrs Clarkson, and Cornevon Lovebird, owned by Mr A. Watt, won fifteen CCs and was Irish Setter of 1974. Her second litter contained four CC winners sired by Sh. Ch. Twoacres Troilus, including Sh. Ch. Cornevon Stargem, best of breed at Cruft's in 1976. Stargem, Lovebird and Love Story were all made up by previously novice exhibitors.

Primrose has now beaten the brood bitch record, held for over forty years by Ch. Norna, by producing nine British CC winning offspring; also four overseas champions.

Somewhat unsure about blowing my own trumpet, I would just add that the Cornevons to date have bred twenty-one British CC winners, plus eight overseas champions.

2

Choosing a Puppy and Basic Training

There are several ways to obtain a well-bred Irish Setter. One is for you to contact the Kennel Club, No. 1 Clarges Street, London, W1 and they will provide a list of Irish Setter breeders in your area. Another useful source is the breed clubs (see Appendix B). Their secretaries can often supply details of litters in various parts of the country. A third way is to buy a weekly dog paper – *Our Dogs* or *Dog World* – which in addition to possibly helpful advertisements contain information about forthcoming shows and breed notes, or apply to the Dog Breeders Associates.

It is a good idea to visit a few shows where Irish Setters are on exhibition. You can walk round the benches and get a close look at the dogs; also you can watch them being judged in the show-ring and perhaps decide which type you prefer. It is a simple matter then to approach the kennel owners and arrange an appointment to view their stock at home.

Any reputable breeder would be delighted to show their adult dogs and older pups if they have any. Bookings from a future litter are generally available on payment of a reasonable deposit.

The question of the pup's sex is best given some thought at this stage. If you are not set on showing, but want a companion/pet then either sex is suitable. Each puppy is an individual character, regardless of whether it is a dog or bitch, they both make affectionate and enjoyable companions. They are like brothers and sisters in a large human family: they are all different but have the same basic characteristics of being affectionate and gay with a tendency to be boisterous when young.

The individual character gradually emerges as each matures. It is true to say that dogs are just as faithful and devoted to their families as bitches but they do take more interest in meeting other dogs when enjoying their daily gallop in parks or fields.

Irish Setters, young ones in particular, are gregarious creatures and love a romp with another dog. In fact, if it is at all possible, the ideal way to keep one Irish Setter really happy is to keep two! However, they are quite content with their human families and adore children.

Reputable breeders normally sell their puppies from about eight weeks old. If you are lucky enough to be able to choose from several pups it is interesting and instructive to watch them playing for a while. Their characters are already forming and it is easy to spot the forward, friendly baby by the enthusiasm shown for your shoe-laces. It can be a mistake to choose a shy pup who may or may not turn out to be nervous. A nervous dog is the first stage towards being an aggressive one. Of course, in experienced and understanding hands, a shy pup can grow up into a normal adult – environment is half the battle and breeding the other half.

Make sure the puppy you choose is bright-eyed and healthy looking, not droopy or dejected, with weepy eyes.

If you are looking for a show dog who is destined to be the foundation of your future stock it is more sensible to buy a bitch. Nobody can be absolutely certain that a promising pup will become a future champion; all sorts of changes take place in a growing dog. Therefore, even if your lovely pup doesn't quite make it as an adult, she is very well bred and can be mated to the best, most suitable stud dog in the country with the prospect of producing your own show-stoppers. But if you have a dog pup which fails to make the grade, the best that can be hoped for is to keep him as a pet and start again.

Ask the breeder if you can see the parents, plus any other members of the family. It should give some idea of how your pup will grow up and what sort of temperament to expect. An Irish should have a gay, extrovert character, friendly to all visitors, people and other dogs alike. They are devoted to their family and probably one member particularly (could it be the hand that feeds and the feet that walk?). They will never forget their friends even if not seen for a long time. On the other hand, if someone leaves the home for only five minutes they get a welcome equivalent to a separation of five days!

Your bitch puppy should be as well bred as possible, with its pedigree including many winner-producing animals; you are more likely to get a good show-dog from parents who are proven good stock 'getters' than from the latest show champion, whose potential is unproven.

The reputable breeder will probably have posed many questions on the suitability of the home you are offering the puppy. Such as 'Is there anyone at home during the day?' Obviously it wouldn't be a very suitable home if everyone was out at work from 9 a.m. till 5 p.m.! The puppy would be terribly lonely and get up to all kinds of mischief simply through boredom. And what happens to the regular four-hourly meals, house-training and the basic general discipline every puppy needs to turn it into a normal adult? Under such conditions your Irish Setter would turn into a destructive rogue with some dirty habits – I might add, through no fault of its own!

Other possible questions are: 'Have you a fenced escape-proof garden?'; 'Do you enjoy long walks in fields etc. in all weathers?' Irish Setters need lots of galloping exercise where they can let off steam and get rid of the high spirits which can be so irritating around the house before they have had their run. A minimum of one hour a day is necessary and they will take as much as you care to give them very happily, once they have stopped growing.

Choosing a promising show pup at about eight weeks old is a combination of experience, luck and 'an eye for a dog'. Possibly you are fortunate enough to possess the last two. However, it would be wise to rely on your reputable breeder's advice on the youngster's faults and virtues, as far as she can see them at such a tender age. Remember, puppies change so much as they grow up and the correct food, exercise and environment are most important.

However, a pup that looks promising at eight to twelve weeks should regain its looks at twelve months after various 'ugly duckling' stages. I stand the puppy on a rubber mat on a table in order to assess it more easily. I look for a miniature version of an adult Irish Setter, minus the coat, i.e. a well-balanced quality puppy with no bad faults. A bitch needs a long, lean head, feminine and pretty, a fine, oval skull, a definite stop and raised brows; the eyes fairly dark with a soft expression; the foreface should balance the skull and have a square finish to the muzzle. A dog should have a stronger, more masculine head, but otherwise similar to a bitch. The teeth should have a scissor bite – an undershot mouth may correct itself with the second teeth but it is not worth the risk. The pup's neck should be long, and arched where it joins the head, set into shoulders that slope well back. A straight front with strong oval bone, and small, tight feet with well-arched toes. The body should be in proportion – well-ribbed back, strong loin and sturdy hindquarters, well-bent stifles and short hocks. The tail should reach the point of the hock.

This is an ideal puppy but obviously the perfect pup has never been bred so just use it as a guide. Coat is practically impossible to assess; generally a pup with a short fine puppy coat will have a straight adult coat but whether it will have sufficient feathering is another matter! A pup with a rough coat will often have a slightly wavy coat with lots of feathering. But there again, sometimes a rough coat turns into a flattish adult coat with excellent feathers. The most promising baby coat is longish and straight, with the beginnings of feathers already present on forelegs, tummy and feet. Another point is colour; a dark brown fluffy coat almost always matures into a darker colour chestnut adult than a paler one.

It is always a help when choosing a puppy to watch them all running around the garden; you can see whether they are moving true or whether there is a tendency to cow hocks or crossing feet. Also when they are playing you can often see their true balance from the side. Don't be too critical. Eight-week-old pups are not very steady and apparent faults are often corrected with good rearing.

Don't forget character and temperament when picking your pup, especially for show. It is so important to have a gay extrovert – a good shower is halfway to that first prize. A bold and playful character may cause headaches in the home but happiness in the ring. A dog which enjoys showing will catch the eye of spectator and judge alike and with responsible training – gentle, firm and regular – will be a joy to handle.

Quality dogs don't grow on trees, however, so be prepared to pay a matching price for a really good promising puppy bred in the purple.

When the decision is made and you have chosen your puppy, the breeder will supply the pedigree, registration, transfer form and, most important, the diet sheet with advice on rearing. I always ask buyers to telephone in a few days with a progress report. I like to keep in touch and help with any problems that may arise. Once the link is established people will keep in contact for years.

My diet sheet at eight weeks is:

BREAKFAST:	½ pint creamy gold top milk mixed with a little Farex or Farlene and Glucose. Also a few biscuits. Plus 3 Vetzymes by hand.
LUNCH:	6 oz minced or chopped meat, mixed with a handful of puppy meal or brown bread soaked in stock a few minutes earlier.
TEA:	As Breakfast.
DINNER:	As Lunch, plus 2 drops of Adexolin and 2 crushed Calcium and Vitamin D tablets mixed in.

Feed Pup every 4 hours.

Variations of protein can be given: shin, ox-cheek, fish, cow beef, horse-meat, rabbit, chicken, eggs and cheese etc.

The amount of food should be **gradually increased** according to the puppy's age, appetite and condition, until, by 5 months old, he should be eating in the region of 1½ – 2 lb meat, 1 pint milk, as much biscuit as he will eat if a **thin** pup, otherwise feed as necessary 4 Calcium and Vitamin D tablets, 8 Vetzymes, 3 drops Adexolin per day. Continue Calcium and vitamins until 12 months.

He will take himself off 'tea' at about 3 – 4 months so add that milk to another meal. He should continue to have a drink of milk for breakfast, plus lunch and dinner, until about 12 months old. An adult needs one small meal in the morning and the main meal at night.

This is a **guide** to what your puppy should be eating. You must judge for yourself according to his appetite and body condition what he needs. A marrow bone is necessary for the puppy to cut his teeth.

INOCULATION at 12 weeks

HOUSETRAINING: Take the puppy out to the garden first thing in the morning; after each meal; when it wakes from a sleep; when it has been playing for a while, and last thing at night. If possible stay with it and give praise when it obliges.

THE BED should be off the floor and out of any draughts.

FRESH WATER should always be available.

MARROW BONES are the **only** safe bones to give and are essential to a teething pup. Also provide its **own** 'toys' – old leather shoes, slippers, a **hard** rubber ball, an old sock for tug-of-war, etc. You can then say 'No' when it takes something it shouldn't.

LEAD TRAINING: Start off gently by putting a very light puppy collar around its neck, not tight, for ½ hour or so each day; gradually lengthen the time until it doesn't cause worry. Attach a light lead to the collar and let the pup lead you. Once it has got used to you holding the lead, you can begin leading the pup. It won't take to it at first but if you coax for just a few minutes at a time it will soon come round. **Don't** drag the pup and don't let children drag it about.

INOCULATION: Ask your vet to come to the house to give the inoculation as the pup might easily catch something while in a waiting room. It can be given at nine and twelve weeks. The vet will give you details.

THE MOST IMPORTANT THINGS for your growing pup are plenty of good food – meat, milk, vitamins, Calcium – also warmth, love, companionship, fresh air and a little discipline. In fact bring up your puppy the same way you bring up your children.

You can stock up your puppy's food and 'bits and pieces' cupboard mainly from Boots – things like Farex (or Farlene, etc.), Glucose, Calcium and Vitamin D tablets, Adexolin drops, Vetzymes, puppy meal, dog biscuits, puppy collar and lead, rawhide dog chews, hard ball etc.

You can add some toys yourself – old socks, knotted, for tug-of-war games and most important, an old soft toy such as a teddy, for the pup's box to compensate for his absent litter companions.

He will need a cosy bed of his own and I recommend a cardboard box with a 'door' cut out of the front as he will chew anything such as a wicker basket at this stage, which can be dangerous. You can put a newspaper in the bottom, and then a piece of old blanket, plus the soft teddy to cuddle up to! The box should be placed in a warm corner where there are no draughts.

If he is sleeping downstairs in the kitchen, he will be rather lonely the first few nights, not having been alone before. If you hear him crying return and sit with him until he goes to sleep, talking soothingly all the while.

The alternative is to take him upstairs to your bedroom and put the box next to your bed. You can be sure of a good night's sleep then as he will be quite content with someone in the room with him. It is less likely that a pup sleeping in the bedroom will have to spend a penny during the night than one alone in the kitchen. The bedroom pup feels secure and sleeps soundly (because he is not alone) whereas the kitchen pup will get out of bed every so often and wander around looking for a companion. Awake, and perhaps cold, it will want to spend a penny.

I always paper-train my pups and so for the first weeks it is safer to put a pad of newspaper down near its bed, just in case of accidents. Unless you actually catch a pup 'in the act' punishment is unwise because the pup will not understand the reason. If it happens before your very eyes, so to speak, then pick him up, reprimand him with the word 'naughty' and put him outside. I have mentioned housetraining in my diet/puppy advice sheet. However, to elaborate a little, it is worth making lots of visits to the garden with your pup and making a lot of fuss of him when he does all that is necessary. He will soon get the idea and know what pleases you.

The first two days of housetraining are the most important; if you can get him into the way of going outside to do his toilet he won't form bad habits of 'spending' in the house. Bad habits are very difficult to break. Should you get a wet patch on a carpet the best way to neutralize the urine and prevent staining is to squirt the area with a soda siphon then mop up with paper towelling.

For general discipline, start as you mean to go on. For instance, if you don't want your pup to occupy the armchairs or settee, say a firm no, right from the start. Perhaps you will make one chair over to him – put a rug on it – and he will soon learn that that chair and no other, is his.

Exercise while young is no problem, as playing in the garden is quite adequate until about the four-month stage. Puppies sleep a lot during the day, just like babies. However, they are a lot more active when awake! The routine goes something like this: asleep – an angelic, cuddly bundle, or a posture suggesting bones of rubber; the awakening – one eye curiously examining the scene, sleepy legs achieving a somewhat drunken stance and then – whoosh – a dynamo of demanding attention. He will probably play for a couple of hours, eat a meal and then sleep again. It's a good idea to have a game in the evening otherwise he'll probably wake up around 2 a.m. full of the joys of spring!

Worming should have been carried out by the breeder. However, it is difficult to completely eliminate worms in a litter as tablets are sometimes brought up again and the breeder doesn't know which pup has been sick. I always worm my pups at least three times before eight weeks but to be quite sure I always give the correct dose of worm tablets to the buyer with instructions on how to use them two days after collection. If the pup passes worms in its motions during the following two days, he should be dosed again with tablets obtained from the vet. The pup can be dosed again when about four months and six months. After that, it should be done when necessary.

You should ask your veterinary surgeon to come to the house

for the first injection against distemper, hepatitus, leptospirosis, when the puppy is twelve weeks old. Don't take him to the surgery; a full waiting room can mean infection flying around and he has no antibodies to protect him. If your vet won't visit, perhaps he has an appointment system. Keep the puppy in the car and then whisk him inside at the scheduled moment. He should not come into contact with strange dogs until a fortnight after the first injection after which he is ready to face the outside world. Until he is fourteen weeks old, he should be confined to the house and garden.

Discipline is very important right from eight weeks as he will get confused if you allow something one day and subsequently scold him for the same misdemeanour. An Irish Setter is very sensitive to your voice and feelings. If you are angry, he will recognize it and be afraid. When he has done wrong and is caught in the act, be 'cross' and tell him what a bad boy he is. He will be very upset and either try to make up to you, or go into his box and sit and tremble until forgiven. You very rarely have to hit a Setter; it hurts them enough to be shouted at. Don't be angry for long – he is only a baby and has a lot to learn. He needs much love and understanding as well as training.

He won't like the car much at first. Pups are often sick because of the motion and noise. The psychological approach is most successful; take him in the car on very short journeys to the local common or park and give him a lovely gallop. He will soon jump into the car with great enthusiasm, knowing a walk is coming. Once he has stopped being travel sick, you can walk him to the fields, if convenient, to get him used to the lead, roads, traffic etc. On long journeys I always give my young stock a Sealegs the night before. They last twenty-four hours and have no side effects and are the best travel-sickness pills I've found.

I have mentioned lead training earlier but it is worth some elaboration. It is important to try to nip in the bud any tendency to pull on the lead. I say 'try' because unfortunately more Setters seem to pull on the lead than not, and they are generally more obedient when loose than on a lead. I think it is because they are so excited by the prospect of a walk; coming home they are usually far more manageable.

To start off with, therefore, it is better to lead train your pup yourself and not let the children take him (unless they are of an age to be strong and sensible). When you are walking with him, don't let him pull away; stop walking and jerk the lead so that he is by your side. Use the word 'heel' so that he associates the command with walking near you. Then start walking again with a fairly loose lead. You may have to do this several times but it is well worth making the lesson understood.

Training a pup to return when called is comparatively easy provided you begin soon enough. Train him in the garden and make it fun with tit-bits and praise when he obeys. Do not make a lesson last more than five minutes as he will get bored and disinterested. If he does well a couple of times, make a big fuss of him and then leave it for the day. Put on your happy voice when calling him to you – get down on your knees and hold out your arms, he won't be able to resist that! He'll come running. Make a great fuss of him and proffer a favourite tit-bit.

When you make your first trip to the local park make sure you are well away from any exits before removing the lead. Take a tit-bit in your pocket and give a piece before letting him loose. It is much safer to let your pup off the lead at the earliest age you can venture out (fourteen weeks) as he is unsure of himself and will stay close for security. Also he isn't big enough to run faster than you! By the time he can you should have him obedient to call.

Basic obedience should start from about eight weeks onwards. A puppy is sensitive to the tone of voice and will react accordingly. If you talk softly, with a happy and caressing tone of voice, he will make a great fuss of you and will come when called. When you say 'No' you must sound as if you mean it! He soon learns what he can and cannot do. If you catch him chewing something forbidden say 'No' firmly and then give him one of his own toys, praising him when he plays with that.

When teaching a puppy to sit, push his rear down while saying 'sit'. Give a tit-bit and praise directly he is in position.

'Stay' is a difficult command for him to learn because he naturally wants to be with you, not at a distance. Ask him to sit and reward him. Then say 'stay' in a firm voice and every time he starts to move push him back and wiggle a finger at him. Only stand a pace away and when he has stayed a few seconds reward and praise him. Gradually extend both the staying period and the distance. Never let the training exceed five minutes (if that) while the pup is still young and never lose your temper. If you begin to feel irritated stop.

When he is about six months, training periods can be extended but never to the extent that the puppy becomes bored and inattentive. Always train by patience and kindness; anything else only frightens the pup.

In my experience Irish Setters generally are not enthusiastic about training school routines. My first dog became quite blatantly bored with an elementary lesson and ended up giving everybody a great laugh by retrieving a dumb-bell and then throwing it up in the air, etc. Obviously the laughter encouraged him. Next time he not only threw the dumb-bell around with gay abandon, he also performed a number of 'bows' slowly lowering his front legs while keeping his bottom high in the air. The message was quite clear. Having grasped the basic exercises, he had become bored by the tedious repitition. Nevertheless, he always remembered the fundamental commands and was most biddable.

If you discover that your puppy is not responding to verbal reprimands as he should then perhaps he is not as sensitive as most Irish Setters. In that case when he has been really naughty (and you must catch him in the act) then either smack him on the rump or shake him lightly by the scruff of the neck while telling him how bad he has been. He will soon learn.

My dogs always know how far they can go with me as when I'm getting cross with them I breathe a deep sigh of exasperation, which they recognize as a danger signal, and stop what they're doing at once. Another device which often works when a pup is getting too excited and won't attend to 'No' is to growl threateningly at them – it always pulls them up short.

'Down' is another very difficult command as they always want to be near your face – they are so affectionate. The only way round this problem is to bend down to his level when he's greeting you. It is instinctive for a Setter to place his feet on your shoulders and give you a big lick – and 'down' is a much-used word when you have a young Setter around the place.

3

The Growing Animal and General Management

I have touched on feeding in the diet sheet in the last chapter but will enlarge on it here as there are so many alternative methods of feeding and it must be confusing to a novice owner.

To have a balanced diet, a Setter needs a combination of protein and carbohydrate. This is normally made up of meat and meal, or one of the proprietary 'all-in-one' balanced dry feeds. There are many different brands of the latter type of food and obviously they must be quite successful with breeds that are good 'doers' and greedy eaters, such as Beagles or Labradors.

However, Irish Setters, especially young, growing animals are often difficult, fussy feeders and some would simply not bother to eat rather than face the same boring dry feed every day. Food is quite low on their list of necessities and youngsters often need variety. They tend to grow at an alarming rate and if they don't eat enough, they soon resemble a walking skeleton. So, if you have a fussy eater, who is mostly skin and bone, check with your veterinary surgeon as a minor ailment can cause lack of appetite. If he is in 'rude' health but doesn't like eating, then the only alternative to a 'boney' is to tempt him.

I know one owner who was still spoon-feeding – literally – her bitch at four years old! But this had just become a bad habit, which should have been broken.

Protein can be fed in a variety of meats, tripe, offal, fish, eggs, cheese and milk. Carbohydrates are a problem with a 'finicky Fred' as he is often persuaded to eat meat but noses the meal out of his bowl! Which makes nonsense of a 'balanced' diet. Luckily, a growing youngster needs more protein than an adult anyway – about two-thirds protein, one-third carbohydrate.

The normal cereal food is either a wholemeal biscuit meal, or an 'all-in-one' type of dry meal, such as Vitalin or Wilsons, to which meat can be added if desired. I use both types of meal, for variety. However, the fussy feeder may turn his aristocratic nose up at these, in which case try other cereals, such as baked brown bread, rice or macaroni cooked with something appetizing like liver or bacon. Other options are rice pudding, fried brown bread, or Farley's rusks.

Large dry biscuits can also be popular. There are many different varieties on the market. My doggy family is very keen on large square wholemeal biscuits and the small yellow ones with added egg.

Dogs can be fed vegetables, although they manufacture a small amount of their own Vitamin C. Many Setters relish raw potatoes and peelings, and sometimes raw carrots. I often cook onions, carrots, in fact, most vegetables, including cauliflower greens and ends of cabbage, etc., with their meat. It makes an appetizing stew – and they eat these chopped up with their meat; the stock is saved to pour over their meal.

They do seem to need to eat coarse grass regularly, and it should be available at some time each day, whether on their walk or in the garden. Sometimes they vomit it back but often it stays down, and is obviously of medicinal benefit.

If an adult will eat a balanced diet, then a vitamin supplement isn't usually necessary. However, the growing animal will need extra calcium and Vitamin D, also a general vitamin and mineral supplement such as Canovel, which is excellent. A bitch in whelp, or feeding pups, also needs the above supplements. A yeast supplement is a good tonic, as is a seaweed preparation.

A normal day's diet for an average adult Setter could be: a handful of dog biscuits (or perhaps a drink of milk or eggs) in the morning after exercise; a main meal at night of meat and meal, about half meat, half cereal, quantity depending on the individual requirements, and age. Young and old dogs usually need two smaller meals, rather than one large one. A youngster of from about six to eighteen months needs more food than an adult of two years and upwards, two main meals, plus milk, eggs and dog biscuits. It is just common sense to decide how much food your Setter needs, depending on his body condition, whether he is fat, thin or just right.

Most dogs adore bones, but the only safe ones are raw marrow bones that don't splinter. If you have several dogs, it might be safer to separate them while they chew – unless you are sure that they won't argue over which bone belongs to whom. Some dogs are real 'magpies', pinching any left unattended and hoarding them in a pile between their feet.

I do believe in toys for them as they tend to get bored with nothing to do all day. Mine have old leather shoes and slippers, knotted socks for tug-of-war, hard rubber balls, rawhide dog chews, etc. The young Setter then has no excuse to chew your carpet or furniture.

Exercise is the next important point. A Setter puppy needs to go and see the outside world every day from about four months to get used to all the strange sights and noises. Cars and lorries are horrifying monsters which can cause youngsters to shy, buck and try to run away so you need a lot of patience to calm the pup, talking gently and stroking it. Acceptance will soon come about.

Taking your youngster shopping is one form of exercise I don't advocate. It's no fun for a pup to be walked through a throng of people, with legs and feet coming from all directions, and then being tied up outside a shop, left alone to shiver and shake, partly through cold and partly anxiety at being abandoned.

You can always go for a short stroll through some quiet street to your local and take the pup in with you; people will make a great fuss of him and he'll soon get used to strangers. But mind he doesn't become an alcholic. Setters tend to like to try anything once!

Real exercise of about an hour's gallop through fields or park is a daily necessity. Start off by taking your three and a half month pup to a nearby common or field for about half an hour. He'll run about fairly near to you and after the first excitement will wander around sniffing at all the interesting new smells. When he's getting tired, he'll walk slowly or sit down and look pathetic. Gradually increase the length of time until at five months he is having around an hour's gallop per day. You can split this up into two or three walks, if you like. Once the pup's about ten months he will take as much exercise as you care to give him – Setters love it.

Road-walking is an over-rated type of exercise. People tell you that if you take your dog for half to one-hour's road exercise per day it will have perfect feet, be in perfect muscular condition and have movement that is out of this world! Take no notice. Half an hour's road work daily probably won't do any harm, but if a Setter did much more regularly it would develop muscles similar to a racing greyhound with large, hard knotted thighs and shoulders which stick out from the body in an unsightly manner. As for feet they are bred, not made.

If you breed from stock with beautiful small, tight feet, then you should have them on your Setters, but if large splayed, ugly feet run in the family, then no amount of road work will help. All you will get is short nails which don't need cutting.

My own Setters have an hour, or more, each day galloping on the local common, which is grass and woodland. They don't get any road-walking but they are born with good feet which remain nice and tight through to old age. The daily gallop builds up their muscles in natural and correct form and keeps them toned up, so their movement is normal.

Feet need checking every day to make sure there are no cuts, thorns or cysts. If it is muddy, or your Setter enjoys digging (as mine do) it is best to wash the mud from between the toes before coming indoors as it becomes rock-hard when dry and is extremely uncomfortable. Some Setters grow nails very fast and these need cutting about every two weeks – just a tiny piece off, making sure you are nowhere near the quick, as that is very painful and rather bloody. Also your Setter probably won't let you anywhere near his feet again.

While grooming you can check the whole dog over for general health and condition. You need two bristle brushes, a coarse one for general brushing and feathering, and a soft one for the face, and to put the finishing sparkle on the coat. I use horse brushes: a dandy brush (coarse bristle) and a body brush (soft bristle). They are large brushes but are ideal for Irish and easier to work with than smaller ones.

The next tool is a steel comb, with a handle. A lotion is very good for the skin and coat, when grooming. I have found Shaw's Coat Dressing excellent; it is water-based and not at all dangerous in regular use. It cleans, deodorizes and repels insects, and also leaves the coat fragrant and shining. I sprinkle a little on the hair and then brush vigorously against the lay of the coat and then back again with it.

Nail clippers are also a necessity. I recommend the square cut nipper variety, as against the guillotine type, which tends to squeeze the nail as it cuts, thus causing the dog more discomfort than necessary.

You will also need various trimming tools for use in show preparation. I will deal with these in Chapter 5.

You now have the basic grooming equipment so we can begin.

I take the steel comb, starting at the root of the tail and comb the hair backwards against the lay of the coat, to the top of the neck, looking all the while at the hair and skin to check for livestock, such as fleas or lice, or for scurf, thorns, and general condition. Having done the back, the sides are next and then the head and ears, following the same procedure.

Having assured myself that he is in clean, healthy condition, I shake the bottle of coat dressing and squirt a few drops into the palm of my hand and then shake it over part of the back (thus ensuring that the hair is only slightly dampened); massage it well in and repeat the process everywhere except the head and face. Then, using the coarse bristle brush, I brush against the lay of the coat (backwards) over the whole of the body, neck and legs; this cleans away any dirt or scurf. Brush the outside of the ears in the same way and the velvet tip of the inside fold, which gets dinner on it! Repeat the process, brushing downwards, with the lay of the coat, so that it's lying flat when finished.

When grooming the feathers on the legs I brush them up towards the body and then try to brush downwards a few strands of hair at a time in order to remove any tangles. Then I comb through the coat and feathers to check for any remaining knots.

The last stage of grooming is with the soft bristle brush. Starting with the face, I brush gently, being careful to avoid the eyes, and then follow the lay of the coat downwards from head to tail, long smooth strokes, putting a polish on the Setter's beautiful coat. Wipe round the eyes with damp cotton wool, checking that there is no inflammation; the same applies to the ears. If there is anything wrong with them, it is best to get your veterinary surgeon's advice on treatment. Check teeth and gums for tartar and inflammation.

If you are going to show your youngster, it is always good training to stand him in a show pose for a few seconds, after grooming is completed. This can be done right from eight or nine weeks old and will, in the beginning, get him used to standing still and being handled, and having his teeth looked at. As he gets older, the stance can be improved as he gets used to the idea. Never spend more than a couple of minutes standing him otherwise he will get bored and naughty. When you have finished give him a tit-bit and praise.

Car-training is something else that needs to be started while the pup is young. Once he has had his second distemper injection, he can go out into the world. We have found that the best way to get a Setter pup used to the car is to take him just round the block for a few minutes finishing up at the local park for a romp. Setters adore their gallops and he will quickly associate the car-ride with the walk at the end of it. Never take a puppy out in the car immediately after a meal, however, as he will probably be sick. A good time is an hour or so before the next meal is due (while still on the four meals a day routine).

Once your Setter has grown out of his baby collar and lead, he will need an adult set. I have found a nylon slip (or choke) collar is ideal for training them not to pull on the lead. I would advise against a choke-chain as the metal will cut the coat and he will end up with an unsightly yellow mark around the neck. Nylon or leather chokes are equally good. Another collar is necessary for normal and show wear. I would suggest a rolled leather collar as ideal as again this will not mark the neck in the way of a flat leather collar. To fit a collar comfortably and safely, you should be able to get two or three fingers (depending on the size of your hand) between the collar and the neck, so that there is some slack but not enough for the collar to be pulled over the ears and head. A dual purpose lead is a strong chain with a leather handle and a safe catch. This can be used both for walks and as a bench chain at shows. Alternatively, there are excellent nylon and leather leads, both suitable, and for the shows you can buy a special benching chain.

Different extremes of temperature and weather can affect a Setter's temperament and comfort. For instance, in the summer if we are lucky enough to have some hot sunshine, Noël Coward's song 'Mad dogs and Englishmen go out in the mid-day sun' is very apt – at least, as far as dogs are concerned. Any normal dog would prefer to doze in the shade during the heat of the day.

Exercise is best given in the cool of early morning and evening. This also applies to feeding as Irish tend to lose their appetites when it is very hot.

A youngster that needs several meals each day could have his main meals as breakfast and evening dinner with milk for lunch. Both shade and sunshine should be available, as sunshine is very good for dogs' health, as well as human beings'.

Cold winter weather is very invigorating and Setters love it. Even old ones romp in the snow and they all have super appetites. However, once they have stopped playing and sit down, they start to shiver and can catch a chill, so always bring your youngster in after a gallop. If it is snowing you must thoroughly dry him and remove the balls of snow which collect between the toes and on the feathers.

Irish Setters loath wet weather. If it's 'down the garden – spend pennies' time, they poke their heads outside the door and run straight back to their beds. However, they need their regular hour's gallop whatever the weather and they don't object to the rain when it's 'walkies' – they hunt as happily as ever. But when they get home you have never seen such poor miserable, underprivileged creatures! They stand with their heads hanging, the picture of dejection. So the first thing is to get a couple of rough towels and dry them off. Then keep them in a warm place until completely dry. Here again, if you have a setter sitting around wet, he is more likely to get a bug than in frosty, dry weather which seems more healthy.

Taking a Setter on holiday is very enjoyable. They are like us in that they love a new place; new smells and fresh walks give even an old dog a new lease of life. When we are holidaying in England we always take two or three dogs with us. They are good company and it makes us take more exercise than we might otherwise. We usually take the old favourites and perhaps a young one; the youngster learns a lot from the older ones – how to behave in strange houses and in cars etc. and it is a good general education, with so many strange people and places.

Some Setters like the sea and splash about trying to catch seagulls – they all adore a run on a long beach, putting up the gulls. They don't all like the sea. Some walk around the edge looking disgusted.

Our first dog, Coppernob, was somewhat bemused when he

first saw us go for a swim in the sea. He ran to and fro along the beach and then took the plunge. At first he swam bolt upright, panicking, his front feet coming clear out of the water, creating innumerable waves and little forward movement. Then he began an efficient dog paddle, heading straight to where we stood waist-high in the water. Unfortunately for us, he decided to climb on to our shoulders. Subsequently we learned to keep out of the way of those flailing claws before he – by now, happily – swam around and returned to the beach.

His son, Snowstorm, always used to scare us in a different fashion – by trying to scale the sheerest of cliffs. There was obviously more interesting sport, like rabbits and mice, and the beach became rather dull. He was extremely surefooted but nevertheless every excursion invoked a quick reaction from us.

There is a place we used to go to in Devon which was ideal for the dogs: a grassy car park on which grazed completely blasé sheep who ignored dogs, cars and people alike. Very good training for young dogs! Leading off towards the sea were sand dunes and then a huge beach, around which ran a twelve foot cliff topped by a large grass, heather and bramble field. The dogs would run up the gently sloping cliff and spend the day hunting rabbits.

Our Setters have stayed in hotels, farmhouses, rented cottages etc. and have never proved an embarrassment to us. They sleep in the bedroom on our rugs and we are always near if they want something. We feed them out in the garden usually, either on tinned meat and meal that we take with us, or else we find a good local pet shop for fresh meat. We always take spare rugs and several towels for drying them off. They become seasoned car travellers in no time.

Remember experiences on holidays are often completely fresh to your pet. Once one of our dogs was absolutely transfixed by sheep appearing near where he was spending a penny. Rooted to the spot, he shook from head to tail and, although he was totally obedient, we quickly put him on the lead and ever after kept him well away from temptation. Better safe than sorry.

Another time we were travelling in an open sports car – something we would never do now. Anyway we had to stop at a level crossing and, as the train roared past, we heard a strange splashing sound. There was six-month-old Pluto standing in the back of the car, watching this strange, noisy monster hurtle past and losing control of his water works at the same time!

Once we were feeding the dogs at late evening in a car park. Suddenly, whoosh, one of the dogs shot off and the next moment was barking excitedly around a passing priest. She had been surprised by his long black cloak and hat; he had probably not danced so energetically for a long time.

It is a sensible idea to insure your dogs. There are insurance companies that specialize in insuring dogs and livestock, and have various terms of cover. At the very least you should insure against third party claims as under the Animals Act the dog owner is liable. So never allow your Setter to walk on a public road without a lead – so many accidents are caused by dogs darting across the road after another dog or cat. It only has to happen once and it is not worth the risk.

Where to house your Irish Setters depends on your personal circumstances and how many you own.

I keep up to half a dozen Irish and they all live in the house as part of our family. Through trial and error we found six the right number. More than that and my husband's asthma and my hay fever have been aggravated by the extra dust and hair the dogs shake out. This is only during the winter when the central heating is on and most of the windows are closed. Also, I found that I was for ever hoovering and polishing to keep on top of the dust and hair. Irish Setter hair is a funny thing – you rarely see it on the carpet or furniture and yet the hoover is always packed tight with it! In the summer the problem doesn't arise as the dogs (and ourselves) spend much of the time in the garden.

Another reason for not having above six Setters is that I found exercising more a problem. I can take six on leads to the common quite comfortably but even one extra makes it a struggle. The more there are, the more excited they become and the more they pull (it's difficult to heel train six exuberant Setters at once). Admittedly, once they're in the common and off the lead they are obedient and manageable – and they are always quieter on the way home.

Then again, my smaller number makes looking after them (feeding, grooming, exercise etc.) more of a pleasure and less of a chore. They need individual attention; being talked to, loved and petted is important to them. When I had a larger number I was too busy and felt too tired most of the time to bother with extra attentions.

We have converted three small rooms into dog-rooms. One is off the kitchen and opens straight into the back garden – a facility very useful in 'dirty paws' weather. They can also sleep there in the summer if necessary; there is too much glass for it to be warm enough in winter. The second one is a small utility room where we have four dog beds. It contains central heating pipes and is very cosy. It also opens into the kitchen and provides a fair amount of space for a bedroom-dayroom for young stock and any puppies that I may be running on for a while. The third room is upstairs and is called the 'nursery' for obvious reasons. My puppies are born there and stay for two or three weeks until they are ready to go outside into the puppy-house.

The youngsters spend most of their day in the kitchen-dog-rooms part of the house and out in the garden; the oldies lie around on the settees. In the afternoon or evening when I go into the sitting rooms the young ones come too – along with a few of their toys to keep them out of mischief.

We have a large double garage made of concrete blocks, and have converted the rear portion into the puppy-house.

Experience plus advice fashioned our present arrangements. Some may prefer to build a puppy place; others may adapt a shed. Essentially, the result must be draught-proof, warm and easy to clean. My husband is quite pleased with our puppy-house and feels it will stand comparison with a purpose-built unit.

Only one wall had to be provided, cutting it off from the rest of the garage. Sheets of plywood are fixed on two sides of 2 × 2 in. frames giving an insulation gap between the two thicknesses. The door, which is in the garage to retain warmth, opens into the puppy-house to reduce the chances of lively pups escaping as you enter. It is a stable door enabling people to look in without pups rushing out.

The walls are lined with thick chipboard and – halfway – with formica. The latter was added after it was found necessary to re-paint the interior after every litter. Now a quick wash down ensures it is sparkling clean at all times. The thick plywood ceiling is covered with fibreglass attic lagging to prevent draughts between joints and vinyl has been stuck to the floor to enable easy cleaning and warmth. Make sure it is stuck completely and sealed at the edges to stop water and urine pooling in inaccessible places.

A small dog-door (2 × 1 ft) leads to the run and there are two infra red lamps and an electric light. It is better to have the light switch separate from the supply to the infra red lamps as a late-night check could have terrible consequences if you switched off the light and lamps at the same time.

Finally – the sleeping quarters. This consists of a huge wooden box (52 in. wide, 38 in. high and 40 in. deep) again lined with vinyl and hardboard. The door which is half the width of the box has a cut-out section (17 × 27 in.) with an edging board to allow the bitch out during the litter's early stages. Later this is removed, the door swung back and a thick blanket dropped in its place. The roof is divided and hinged so that an infra red lamp can be lowered inside. Secure the door blanket firmly as the inevitable tug-of-war with the trailing edge can displace a housebrick, etc. with dire results!

The run should be quite large (ours is 4 × 6 yds) securely fenced and with a concrete run sloping to a soakaway. It should also be in the area likeliest to get the most sunshine. Our run is bounded by plastic coated chain link with boards at the bottom to prevent pups pushing underneath and at the top to avoid bending when the pups are old enough to jump up. The gate to the run opens inwards and there is a plank on its edge just inside to stop the pups coming out when we do. Incidentally, the small door to the puppy-house has a conventional door catch to allow it to be opened or shut from either side. Use the rounded handle though as puppies quickly master the lever type and could get shut out during the night.

A word of caution. On particularly cold winter nights people have been known to supplement puppy-house heating with a paraffin stove. Invariably, this is accompanied by shutting windows and plugging door gaps. Such a situation has lead to the puppies being very ill because the available air becomes heavily laden with fumes.

My own preference is to keep Irish as housedogs rather than in kennels as they are a breed that thrives in human company. Also, they are calmer and easier to manage if they have been used to having people about them. You only have to visit an average kennel where the dogs live in kennel and run, except for exercise periods, to see – and hear – the difference. They become so excited they bark and leap up at the wire. When let out they charge about, leaping on anyone present and generally creating havoc. When they are put back, they look so unhappy at being imprisoned again.

If it is imperative to keep your dogs outside, please ensure that they all spend some time in the house every day as they need human company as much or more than anything else.

Before I married, my family kept a boarding and breeding kennel for a few years and in the summer we sometimes looked after up to fifty dogs at once. There was a time when we owned twenty dogs – a few Irish but mostly beagles belonging to my mother and sister.

We lived in a small bungalow and naturally couldn't keep that number inside so all but the half-dozen privileged ones were kennelled, at night anyway. We had two acres of field and bush and during the day (when it was fine) they had this area to play in. Needless to say, whenever one of us came outside the dogs were sitting around the back door hopefully. They all had turns in the house, and were fairly happy, until it came to bedtime when we tucked them up snugly in enormous straw beds – two or three to a kennel for company and warmth – and gave them their good-night 'bickies'. Then they would gaze mournfully at us as if we were doing them a terrible injustice. I used to feel miserably guilty and vowed that when I had my own home they would all sleep in the house, if not the bedroom. (I've always had the two oldest in the bedroom.)

Incidentally, I found that having a lot of dogs did not make me more successful. It just meant a lot more mouths to feed. We live in a time when it is terribly expensive to keep, breed and show dogs and most people cannot afford to show more than two or three at once. Breeding should be for quality, not quantity, to improve your strain – not to mate that pet bitch just because she is in season. So you see large numbers of dogs aren't necessary or desirable.

My ideal establishment – who hasn't one? – would be a large house in the country with half a dozen acres of meadows and trees, all securely fenced, where the dogs could hunt and play without any worries about what the local gamekeeper might say when the Setters put up pheasants, chase rabbits and dig enormous holes.

I would have about four dog-rooms downstairs; all opening on to the garden, furnished with dog-beds and benches. A couple of the rooms would have old, washable leather settees and armchairs, and perhaps a television to turn it into a shabby sitting room for me and the dogs. Of course, there would also be normal reception rooms including a posh lounge with a notice on the door saying 'No dogs admitted'. This would be for such rare visitors who prefer smart clothes to friendly dogs. There would be an indoor nursery for the new families, and two or three super outside puppy-houses and runs, custom-built, with all mod cons. Ah well, we can always dream.

Back to earth again. If you have several dogs it is necessary to walk around your dog garden with a bucket, shovel and scraper every day. It is also a good idea to throw down a bucket of disinfectant on heavily used areas once or twice a week – more often in summer.

Irish Setters generally prefer your bed or the settee. However, when these are not available, they'll settle for a large basket, preferably big enough for two (they love to snuggle up together); or a Goddard dog-bed which is a steel frame on legs. Three of the sides are fitted with washable cotton covers, the fourth is open and the floor is canvas. Alternatively, the dogs don't mind wooden benches with an end board along the sides to hold in the bedding. I usually place newspapers underneath with blankets on top.

The benches are generally used as daytime loungers and I cover these with carpet pieces. They have a dual purpose because they are most useful when it comes to grooming and trimming. Trained from puppies, they will stand on the benches while being brushed – and it saves a lot of backache!

4
Breeding

Breeding is like Hampton Court maze – take the wrong turning and you can be a long while finding the right path. A most helpful book for the beginner is Eleanor Frankling's *Practical Dog Breeding and Genetics*.

There are many factors to be taken into account. To begin with, you must be sure that your foundation bitch is sound and well-bred, of good quality, strong and healthy, and with no serious faults. For instance, a nervous bitch should not be used as nervousness frequently becomes aggression in a frightened animal: it bites because it is afraid. This fault is passed on to the offspring.

Other failings can be an undershot mouth or a poor, weedy animal without enough bone or general stamina. No thought should be given to breeding with a dog which has, or is a carrier of, a serious hereditary fault.

Ideally the bitch should be between two to three years old for her first litter but it doesn't normally harm an Irish Setter to have her first litter at a more mature age provided the veterinary surgeon considers her fit and able to produce comfortably. Irish Setters, for their size, have rather small, long, thin puppies with proportionate heads so that a normal whelping is a fairly easy, safe affair.

No Setter bitch should be mated under eighteen months. I personally consider two years quite young enough, as many, up to this time, remain immature, both mentally and physically. However, some mature more rapidly than others and you must judge for yourself which type you have, and act accordingly.

Although you are probably keen to breed a litter do consider all that it involves before reaching a final decision. Many people believe that their bitch should have one litter for her health's sake. This is nonsense, as a bitch which has had several litters is still as likely to have pyometra or metritus as a maiden bitch. There are extremely maternal bitches which have false pregnancies after every season and still do, after a litter. Then again you might think that if you breed a litter of Irish Setters you will make a lot of money when you sell them. This is just a pipe-dream.

The expense of breeding a litter of Setters, from conception to the age when you can (hopefully) sell the pups, is considerable.

It is also important to think about the time involved. The puppies will arrive nine weeks after mating and will be ready to go to their new homes eight weeks after birth. They will need a great deal of time and hard work. It is as well to be pessimistic in planning your budget and work schedule as you may still be caring for unsold puppies three to four months after they were born. Food will be a great expense as growing Setter puppies need an increasingly large amount of good food; also veterinary surgeon's bills must be taken into account, plus inoculations at twelve weeks.

Apart from the extra time and money involved in breeding a litter, the housing and heating requires careful thought. It is both convenient and pleasant to have the litter born and reared for the first two to three weeks in the house – but the bitch and pups must have a quiet room of their own, undisturbed by the general hustle and bustle of the household. It is so much easier when you want to check that all is well, just pop your head around the door, instead of going out of the house, through the garden and into the puppy-kennel. Of course, this will come later when the pups are older, and outside, but it won't be as necessary to keep such a close watch on them after the first two weeks.

The room indoors, the nursery, as I prefer to call it, requires a whelping box about 3 × 4 ft or larger; three sides about 18 in. high with the fourth side hinged for when the pups are old enough to walk out. Ideally, it should be lined with vinyl, sides and bottom, for easy cleaning. A movable bar can be fitted about three inches from the floor and protruding about the same distance from the sides to prevent very young pups from being squashed if their mum is careless when lying down.

Most Irish are very careful when getting in with their babies but you occasionally get an awkward one. I once lost a newborn pup during the night. It had been squashed flat but it wasn't

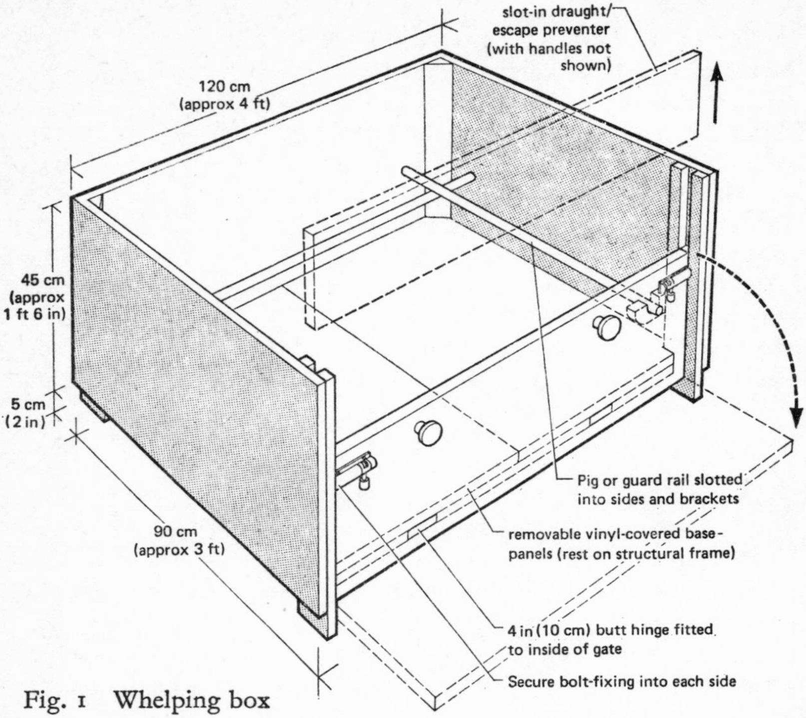

Fig. 1 Whelping box

mum's fault as we found she had developed quite a high temperature and didn't know what she was doing.

The rail can be removed after the first few days when dam and babies are accustomed to each other.

The next necessity is warmth. Newborn pups need a temperature of around 75°F. (23·9°C.). If the room temperature is 70°F. (21·1°C.) the warmth of the dam will increase the proximity temperature to 75°F. (23·9°C.). I have two sources of heat in my nursery – a radiator and a Wren Foster infra-red lamp, dull emitter. Suspended by a chain over one half of the whelping box it can be raised or lowered according to the warmth required. The lamp should never be lower than six inches above the bitch's back when standing. These lamps are very economical and quite safe, if used correctly.

A third method of heating which has been recommended to me but which I have yet to use, is an electric pad, fitted with a soft waterproof cover and placed in the whelping box under a false floor for safety. It should be set on a very low temperature. The pad can be used in conjunction with a room heater maintaining a general room temperature up to 70°F. (21·1°C.). If you have to use a floor standing heater make sure it is screwed to the ground. I would not use a paraffin heater because of the fumes (once, during a bitter wintry night, I checked and found the bitch and pups wheezing because of the oppressive atmosphere). If such heating is essential – through strikes, power cuts etc. – then make absolutely sure there is ample ventilation while keeping the temperature to the required level.

A final word on the nursery. Vinyl is an ideal flooring material as it is easy to keep clean and hygienic.

A modern, very effective way of keeping pups warm and dry is Vetbed, a man-made fleecy blanket which allows any moisture to drain through, whilst staying warm and dry on top. It is machine-washable and dries in a few hours.

Choice of stud dog

Choosing a husband is not easy (when was it ever!) You would be well advised to consult your bitch's breeder, who will know her background and will probably have some idea of what might suit her. Never use the dog down the road for convenience' sake; he is probably quite unsuitable with nothing to recommend him but availability! After all, the object of the exercise is to improve the breed.

This is a good time to visit some championship shows if you haven't already been exhibiting at these. You can study the dogs and look up the sires of the ones you like. This way you may find a good sire with the right bloodlines to combine with your bitch. Also check on her faults and virtues to ensure you are not doubling up on undesirable points.

Inbreeding should be avoided by a novice breeder as you need to know exactly what lies behind your stock, and both parents must be as near perfect as possible from the physical, mental and genetic aspects. Inbreeding is the mating of father to daughter, brother to sister etc. By so doing, you fix both faults and virtues and also uncover factors not apparent.

Line breeding is the mating of two distantly related animals of the same strain and is safer in that you are not concentrating on two or three dogs but have a much wider range of ancestors.

Outcrossing is the mating of two un-related animals and unless one of the parents is dominant for type, anything can result: a mixed bag. However, it is possible to breed together two dogs from unrelated, but well-established blood-lines, and produce excellent animals if a 'nick' has taken place. In other words, the parents luckily suit each other and the ensuing progeny are good specimens.

My own Irish began in this way: two almost unrelated Setters which, bred together, produced my first show champion and his lovely sister who bred me four more show champions in two litters. If you start off with this method and the results are good, you can then linebreed to outstanding animals on one side of the pedigree and thus begin your own strain.

For this method to be successful you must have an excellent and prepotent (that is, dominant for good qualities) parent and be lucky enough to get a 'nick'. Otherwise it is a hit-or-miss method and even if you get an outstanding specimen, there is no guarantee that it will pass on its good points to its progeny.

Perhaps linebreeding in an established and typical bloodline is the method more likely to bring good results. Always remember that a breeder should be striving to improve his stock with each subsequent generation. Anyhow, at the beginning of your breeding activities it is often wise to ask your Setter's breeder for advice on choice of stud dog.

Mating

Having decided which dog is suitable for your bitch, you then contact his owner. The stud dog owner is entitled to ask various questions about your bitch, pedigree and your facilities for the coming litter. He may also like to see the bitch before accepting her as a mate for his dog. If a bitch of poor type produces an inferior litter to his dog, it could harm the sire's reputation. If all is well, you arrange to contact him as soon as your bitch comes in season to give a rough idea when she will need mating. Be sure to establish the stud fee.

Your Setter should be in good condition, not too thin or fat, with a shining coat and good muscles. About the time she is due in season, check her vulva daily for colour and swelling. When she starts bleeding notify the stud dog owner, giving a possible date for the mating but leaving it fairly elastic until you see that she is ready to stand. Then confirm the day.

For about the first ten days of season, her vulva will swell up and be hard; then gradually it will become soft and flabby, although still enlarged. Her coloured discharge may change from a dark red to a pale straw colour as the time of mating draws near but some bitches go on showing strong colour right up to the last few days of heat and this does not signify there is anything amiss.

Bitches vary from one to another, and from season to season, as to when they are ready to be mated. I have had a bitch conceive a small litter from an accidental mating on her eighth day but larger litters tend to stem from later matings, between about the twelfth and sixteenth days, depending always upon when the bitch starts to stand. Normally, standing goes on for about five days and obviously mating should take place during this time.

The easiest way of deciding when your bitch is ready is to watch her reactions to another friendly bitch. She will arch her tail to one side, and back into the other's face, hoping to be mounted, and if they are pals, they will play sexy games, mounting each other (We always said some of our old girls would have made superb stud dogs!). Such goings-on are quite normal for bitches in season.

If you have no other bitches, you can get a reaction by scratching the root of her tail or touching her vulva. She will arch her tail and brace her back legs and if her vulva is soft and flabby, she should be ready for mating.

Having made all the arrangements, set off in the car in plenty of time so that on arrival you can take her for a short walk to relieve herself and relax after the journey.

When people bring a bitch to one of my dogs I like the occasion to be as natural and happy as possible. When the bitch has relieved herself and been offered a drink, I then bring the dog and bitch together in the garden – on a lead if the bitch is put out by the appearance of a strange dog. Once they have been introduced, I unleash them and let them have a romp in the garden. The collars stay on but the romp will relax the bitch and put her in a happier state of mind for the actual mating.

If the weather is fine, and it is convenient, the mating can proceed in the garden. However, if jolly jinks on the lawn make the neighbours boggle-eyed, the garage or dog-room are best adjourned to before the courting becomes too serious.

It is often frightening for a maiden bitch to be taken to a strange place and an enthusiastic unknown dog. She may growl or snap at him, so take your time. If he courts her and plays, she will soon like him. But if he is one of the no-nonsense type and wants to get straight on with the matter in hand, she may still be frightened and growl. At this stage, her collar should be firmly grasped by her owner so that she does not turn her head and bite the animal that wants to serve her.

You will soon know if she is ready to be mated because, even if she growls at him, when he mounts her she will turn her tail to one side and brace herself to take his weight. If she is not ready she will sit down or struggle and may need another couple of days before trying again.

Of course, a bitch who has had a litter and knows the ropes will probably be quite good-humoured and placid about the whole thing.

One of my champion bitches went to stay at the home of the stud dog as I was out of the country at the time. The owner, a close friend, told me later that after the first mating – which the bitch enjoyed – every morning she would go down to his kennel run and call for him – it was a real love-match.

I don't believe in forcing a mating. Some bitches are so reluctant that they struggle and fight to get away, throwing themselves about bodily, so that it is practically impossible for the dog to mate her. The reason for this might be that she is not ready, or perhaps she is past her peak time; or she may simply be terrified. If it is the third reason, it could be worthwhile to rest her until the next day when she might be less afraid.

In these cases it might take three people to hold her and assist the stud dog. A terrified bitch that growls and tries to bite the dog should never be forced; it is very unkind to tie her mouth as some people do. It is probably best to forget about mating her and make new plans. Mating should be a natural, enjoyable time for the dog and bitch.

When a dog mates a bitch, a tie usually results, which holds them together for anything from five to sixty minutes. This tie is caused by the dog's penis swelling quite considerably inside the

Cribarth Maydream, aged seven weeks (*Michael Oakley*)

Cornevon Oberon and Cornevon Westerhuys Cloggy, aged nine weeks (*Michael Oakley*)

Sh. Ch. Wendover Gentleman (19 CCs). Best-in-Show Hove Championship Show 1969 and one of the top sires of all time (*Sally Anne Thompson*)

OPPOSITE:

Sh. Ch. Twoacres Troilus (21 CCs). Irish Setter of the Year 1971, Stud dog of the Year 1974, 1975 and 1976

Sh. Ch. Cornevon Primrose (17 CCs). Irish Setter of the Year 1970 and 1972, holder of the Brood Bitch record of all time (*Piet Jacobs*)

Ch. Astley's Portia of Rua, Supreme Champion, Cruft's, 1981 (*Michael Oakley*)

Sh. Ch. Scotswood Barabbas (*Piet Jacobs*)

Sh. Ch. Cornevon Primrose (*left*) handled by the author and Sh. Ch. Wendover Caskey handled by Mr. R. Heron, judged by Mr. W. J. Rasbridge (*centre*) as his two CC winners at Richmond Championship Show 1969

vulva and being held there by the bitch's contracting vagina. Once the tie is evident the dog will unclasp his forelegs from around the bitch's body and get down and turn around. Assistance can be rendered by lifting one foreleg over the bitch's back, so that both front legs are together, and then raising the corresponding hind leg gently over the bitch's hindquarters. It sometimes happens that when turning the dog, the bitch will cry out in pain. Once the dog has turned, they should be standing comfortably back to back on all four feet. The handlers should hold on to their collars to prevent them dragging each other about – or trying to lie down! If the bitch is upset and crying or drooling, the owner should talk gently to her, giving her confidence.

It is of great benefit at this stage for the handlers to have something to sit on – half an hour at the crouch can do some excruciating things to previously unheard-of muscles.

When the mating is over, the bitch should be removed to a quiet place for a while; if she has travelled by car, she will be content to rest there after the offer of a drink.

If the mating was straightforward and successful, your bitch won't require a second service. But, if there is any doubt, then a second mating within forty-eight hours should suffice.

The stud fee should be paid after the service and most owners will offer a free mating at her next season if the bitch has no pups. The stud dog owner should give you a receipt containing the date of mating, the stud dog's registration number and a copy of his pedigree.

Be very careful not to let your bitch get out to another dog for the rest of her season, or she might produce a mixed litter.

Pregnancy

The normal term of pregnancy is nine weeks, give or take two or three days either way. Your bitch should enjoy her normal routine for the first few weeks. She should have been treated for roundworms before she was due in season. However, it is safe to worm an in-whelp bitch up to three weeks after mating, using roundworm tablets obtained from your veterinary surgeon.

Exercise is vital during pregnancy for the health of both bitch and unborn puppies. A Setter is a galloping dog and there is no reason why she should not continue to enjoy a free run right up to the day she whelps. As her body becomes heavier, so she will gradually slow down to a more becoming pace until for the last week or two she will be ambling along at a sedate pace, suitable to a matronly lady.

Years ago, when my old foundation bitch was due to whelp any day, she came on our daily walk quite happily, apparently without a care in the world. When we got home she went back to bed for a rest, and when I looked in on her an hour later, she was washing her first whelp! She looked at me in a very saucy manner, obviously saying, 'Aren't I clever! How about a drink of milk?' Of course, she was an experienced mum, who felt very fit and never made a fuss about whelping. Most young bitches, expecting their first litter, give ample warning, anything from twelve to thirty-six hours before they actually give birth.

To get back to pregnancy, her food intake should be normal until the fourth week, as long as it contains at least 50 per cent meat, plus a good quality cereal, and a vitamin and mineral supplement.

As she gets heavier, probably around five weeks pregnant, her food should be divided into two smaller meals, and the protein (meat etc.) should be increased. Don't increase the cereal, as bulky meals will make her uncomfortable, and she needs concentrated nourishment at this time of pressure on the abdomen. If she becomes very heavy around seven weeks, give her three smaller meals per day.

Apart from her staple diet of meat, tripe, heart and liver could be added with advantage. An ounce or two of liver every day is excellent, full of vitamins, and will keep her motions a little softer, which is a good thing as it is bad for her to get constipated when she is heavy in whelp, and straining is so uncomfortable. However, too much liver will give her diarrhoea which must also be avoided. Bones also cause constipation, so cut them out until after whelping.

A daily helping of egg and milk is very nourishing also. Her calcium intake should be increased from the fourth week. There are several different ways to give calcium, depending on how your bitch will take it. A balanced product where you have the right proportions of calcium, phosphorus and vitamins, is probably the simplest method. For example, Stress is a suitable product, specially made for bitches and puppies. You add this powder to the food. However, some bitches refuse to eat doctored meals so the answer then is tablets, put down her throat by hand. Calcium and Vitamin D tablets, as mentioned in my diet sheet, are excellent, giving perhaps two tablets twice a day. You must add to her diet either a single multivitamin supplement, such as Canovel tablets; or Adexolin drops or cod liver oil for Vitamins A and D, plus a yeast supplement such as Vetzymes, for the Vitamin B constituent.

I have stressed that your bitch needs a large supply of good protein food – possibly twice her normal allowance – but don't fall into the trap of letting her get fat. She must be fit, not fat. Most of her extra food is going into nourishing her babies, not turning her into a Bessy Bunter.

Preparations for Whelping

At least a couple of weeks before the puppies are due, it is a good idea to accustom your bitch to her whelping quarters for a while each day, and encourage her to have a nap in the whelping box and perhaps feed her in it. Familiarity will make her more secure about producing her family in it.

It is inadvisable to let her sleep alone at night for the last week of pregnancy. In fact, for the whole of this final week she should be with a responsible person both day and night, in case she decides to produce her family early. More often than not a bitch will spend the day making beds, digging holes and generally puffing and blowing – only to go to sleep in the evening. This can lull you into a feeling of false security and you go to bed thinking she's shelved the idea until tomorrow – only to be woken in the middle of the night by a Setter sitting on your chest saying, 'Help, I'm starting.'

Many bitches prefer to have their family at night, when it's quiet and undisturbed by the daily turmoil.

Whelping

Follow the Boy Scout motto – Be prepared – from the start. Always notify your veterinary surgeon when you see the warning signs described below, just in case you need him in an emergency.

Some Setters carry their pups the full term of sixty-three days or even a day over. Others whelp two or three days early and this is all quite normal.

Very occasionally, a bitch will have her litter up to a week early and the premature pups – away from the warm womb and having to get their own food – will probably cry for twenty-four hours as they struggle to become co-ordinated. Don't be alarmed by their bright red noses and feet. But do take special care to ensure they are really warm and are suckling. Puppies born more than seven days early do not have much chance of survival. Fortunately, this doesn't happen often.

Should a pregnant bitch fail to start whelping by her sixty-fifth day it is advisable to get the veterinary surgeon to check her out. It will make you happier, even though the bitch may look at you as if to say 'What's all the fuss about?'

Warning signs of approaching labour can be seen anything up to thirty-six hours before she actually begins to strain. When you see her digging large holes in the garden, making beds in the house, sitting or lying about panting and washing her front legs, and other parts of her anatomy, and looking generally uncomfortable, then heed this warning and get together the necessities for whelping and place them in the whelping room. Earlier the room should have been cleaned thoroughly, including washing the whelping box with disinfectant, and heated to a temperature of about 70°F. (21·1°C.).

The necessities are as follows: a small pile of clean newspapers, half a dozen clean, rough dog towels, fairly blunt, sterilized scissors, small bottle of ferric chloride (obtainable from veterinary surgeon or chemist), one or two hot water bottles, a packet of glucose, several pints of milk, a large water bowl and a small milk bowl, a teaspoon, cotton wool, pen and paper, a plastic sack and a supply of tea or coffee, and chair, for the midwife!

A bitch's temperature is normally 101·5°F. (38·5°C.) and some hours before whelping this will drop to 98°F. or 99°F. (37°C.). However, unless you are used to taking dogs' temperatures, don't add to the bitch's discomfort. Also I have known expectant mums' temperatures to rise again just before whelping.

Make sure you wash the bitch's undercarriage (including all the teats) and then anus and vulva with shampoo or soap and warm water, and rinse and dry thoroughly. For obvious hygienic reasons, this should be done before the actual straining stage – and after digging up the garden.

During the first stage she will have several periods of sleep between bouts of activity. As whelping approaches she will pant a lot between washing herself and giving worried glances at her rear. It is best to entice her into the nursery then, as straining is imminent. Her whelping box should be covered in several layers of newspaper, which she will probably tear up. If she asks to go out in the garden again, go with her and watch her – she might drop a puppy without realizing when emptying her bowels.

Don't have the nursery too hot before she has produced her first pup as she will be hot enough already. You can switch on the infra red lamp when the pup arrives, if a winter litter.

Second stage labour starts with the actual straining. The panting stops for a moment and the bitch's body heaves and she may groan. Note the time of the first real 'strain' as if she continues straining beyond an hour with no success there may be a complication and you should ask your veterinary surgeon to come out immediately. My veterinary surgeons are marvellous and usually arrive within ten minutes for a whelping emergency. They have stipulated one hour because Setters usually have their puppies easily. Longer could obviously weaken the bitch for the task ahead. A veterinary surgeon will usually put any small trouble right so that the bitch can continue whelping in a strong condition. If the complication is more serious he may take her back to his surgery. Breech births (that is, hind-quarters first) do not normally cause problems. Complications arise when two puppies are presented together, or there is an abnormally large whelp or a pup is doubled up.

As to the birth of the first pup, the bitch will strain every few minutes and when not straining will pant and wash herself and perhaps tear up newspaper. As the whelp progresses down the passages towards the outside world, the heaves become more frequent and the bitch will attempt to lick her vulva (a vigorous exercise for a heavily in-whelp bitch).

The puppy emerges in a cushioning bag of membranes. As the head, enveloped in dark membranes, appears, a maiden bitch may cry out in pain. She will probably be frightened so talk to her reassuringly. When the pup's head is through, the rest will follow quickly and another strain will produce the afterbirth or placenta. The maiden bitch may be bewildered and, not realizing what has happened, ignore the pup and clean up her own hind end. If this happens, the first thing for you to do is to break open the bag – with fingers – at the nose of the puppy to enable it to breathe. If it shows signs of life, put it under mum's nose and encourage her to lick it. Normally, she will eat the afterbirth, chew through the umbilical cord and thoroughly wash the baby – probably in that order. By this time, the pup should be crying, stimulated by the pushing and nosing around that goes with the washing. As it starts looking for the 'milk-bar' you can provide a helping hand by putting it on a nipple.

However, some maiden mums are silly about their first born and have to be shown what to do. So you gently remove the membrane from around the puppy and deal with the umbilical cord yourself. I shred it with my fingers at about two inches from the pup's tummy which seems to avoid any bleeding. An easier method for a novice breeder is to cut it with blunt, sterile scissors, about one and a half inches from the navel; if necessary you can tie it with thread to stop any bleeding. The ferric chloride is invaluable in this instance. Just put a drop on a little piece of cotton wool and dab the end of the cord for a few seconds. This always stops bleeding. After this, take a warm towel and give the pup a good rub all over, drying it thoroughly. If it seems to have liquid mucus still in its lungs – it will be blowing bubbles and be unable to cry or breathe properly – hold if firmly in the towel, one hand under its chest, the other round its head and back, and swing it head downwards a few times. This should make the pup cry and mum might take an interest in it; put it next to her and see if she will lick it. If she is still not sure, talk to her gently while putting it on to a nipple. The suckling, and your soothing words, should soon give her a maternal feeling and she will start to lick it – all is now well. Fill a hot water bottle and wrap it securely in a towel, putting it near the milk-bar and the pup. Wrap the placenta in a newspaper and put into the plastic sack for burning.

Straining is less severe after the first whelp and the next baby may already be on the way. Again make a note of the first contraction, only this time work to a maximum of half an hour of straining before contacting the veterinary surgeon. Mum will probably be able to play an increasing part in coping with the subsequent arrivals.

If possible, remove the wet, stained newspapers from around her hindquarters and replace with dry ones without moving her. The box should be kept as dry as possible as it helps to keep the pups warm. Put the dirty paper into the plastic sack.

Write down the time of birth, sex etc. and also whether the placenta arrived or not. This is necessary and is always of interest later. If the bitch doesn't mind, you can weigh them as well.

After she has finished dealing with each new arrival, I give mum about a quarter of a pint of milk with half a teaspoon of glucose mixed in. This is gratefully received as she is hot and bothered and working very hard.

Puppies always seem to congregate around mum's back end (almost as though they want to go back to the comfort of her womb) so as another is about to be born remove any from there and put them on the wrapped hot water bottles until she has finished with the new one. I give any wet ones a good rub with a towel when the bitch is occupied with another, but she will fret if you handle them too much.

Whelping can take a long time. Many years ago one bitch of mine started producing about 10 a.m. and averaged about one an hour. By 10 p.m. we decided she had finished as there had been nothing for a couple of hours and she had settled down and stopped panting. She had produced ten pups and looked slimmer! At eight next morning a check revealed she had produced four more puppies and was efficiently coping with all fourteen.

Fortunately there had been no complications otherwise we could have lost her and her pups. So we always sleep with our bitches the night after whelping and keep a close eye on them for several days and nights. On the other side of the coin, another bitch had twelve puppies in five and a half hours.

Each whelping is different, even with the same bitch, so it pays dividends to stay with your bitch. In this way I have never lost a bitch whelping and only one puppy was 'sat on'.

Whelping bitches instinctively eat the puppies' placentas as part of the process of giving birth and this helps the milk production. I always let the mum eat half a dozen or so but if it's possible to remove some of the afterbirths without upsetting her, then I do so. They can cause awful diarrhoea for a few days after whelping. Always count the placentas as one retained can bring trouble.

When she has finished whelping, she will settle down happily with her new family, stop panting and go to sleep for a while. She would appreciate a large drink of milk, Farlene and glucose and you could suggest a quick trip to spend pennies. However, don't be surprised if you have to put her on a collar and lead before she will move from her prized possessions. She usually has to feel pretty desperate before she will go out and then she will be back in double quick time. While she is out, clear the box and put in a double thickness of newspaper and a clean piece of Vetbed (which can also be used for the whelping). Change the Vetbed every morning.

If she finishes producing her family during the night and is quite contented, don't call your veterinary surgeon until morning. If it's during the day, you can call him immediately. My veterinary surgeon always examines the bitch to see if she has any more puppies tucked up under her ribs or stray afterbirths left inside. If this is the case, he can remedy the situation. A bitch can become very ill or die from a rotting dead puppy or placenta.

Even when he has examined her and pronounced everything correct, my veterinary surgeon will give an injection of penicillin and pituitrin to be sure. While he is there, you can arrange with him to come and remove the pups' dew claws on about the fourth day.

Care of the puppies

If your litter is a large one it may be necessary to have some put to sleep by your veterinary surgeon. It is sensible to wait until your pups are about four days old before making a decision, as you may lose some anyway – perhaps a weakling, a 'sat-on' casualty, or a virus. This all sounds terribly pessimistic but it can happen, along with other things.

Your bitch can probably manage eight puppies comfortably, and ten at a pinch with early weaning. More than this number and she will need help feeding them. Unless you are lucky enough to have a foster mother on tap, the sensible course is to put some down, although it does seem a shame when they are all perfectly healthy. However, you must bear in mind that a large litter of Irish

Setters costs a fortune to rear properly and it can be very difficult to find the right homes for puppies when you are not very well-known and it is your first litter. You may find yourself still feeding them at four months!

If you want to supplement your bitch's milk I recommend Lactol for the pups. You can use an eye-dropper or a premature babies' feeding bottle. It is not a good idea to constantly feed the same pups, they should all be fed in turn, because the mother's milk is still best.

Some years ago I had three show champion bitches, all around the same age. They would come into season together and when I mated one, the other two always came into milk when the pups were born. They often had large litters of twelve and whichever one wasn't being shown would foster half the litter – most successfully. I used to swop the pups about so that they all had some of their real mum's milk. Also they all stayed with mum for the first few days for the colostrum. The pups reared this way all turned into big healthy youngsters.

Once a London evening paper wanted some pictures for a pre-Cruft's edition and as a result we have now got some lovely photographs of one litter and two 'mums' all in the same enormous compartment!

Make sure that the pups are warm. You can tell by their positions. If cold, they huddle on top of one another in a buzzing squirming heap, pulling their hindlegs underneath them. If too hot, they will spread out by themselves. You need a happy medium, where they sleep contentedly in a row next to mum and the milk-bar.

To alter the temperature you can raise or lower the infra red lamp but remember never have it lower than six inches above the bitch's back when she is standing. It is difficult to get an ideal temperature for both bitch and puppies because the latter have to be kept very warm for the first week. On the other hand, she gets too hot and will probably dig up the bed in an effort to find a cooler spot. Compromise by keeping the lamp over one side of the box so that she can get away from it without leaving the box. I keep a thermometer on the side of the box to ensure the temperature stays around 70°F. (21·1°C.).

Of course, in the summer artificial heat may not be necessary: in heatwaves it has been a problem to keep dam and babes cool enough! Room temperatures over 80°F. (26·6°C.) can cause heat exhaustion. I have overcome this difficulty by putting mum and litter outside on the grass in the shade of a big tree in our enclosed (and separate from the dogs') garden, occasionally damping the puppies' heads and faces with a cold, wet towel.

Contented pups don't cry – they give an occasional gurgle or squeak but nothing more.

If one or more pups continually cry there is something amiss. Where there is no obvious cause, call in the veterinary surgeon. There could be something wrong with the bitch's milk or the pups themselves. Puppies can get tummy upsets from their mother's milk – a diarrhoea bug perhaps – and will need medicine. If the bitch continues to have bad diarrhoea for several days she should have veterinary treatment.

One of my bitches unfortunately developed colitis a couple of weeks before she whelped, and she was treated for some time before and after whelping. It was a bad time to have it as she and the puppies needed a great deal of nourishment and, of course, she was not eating well.

She whelped eleven pups which were not all as big and strong as usual, and with their first taste of her milk the pups caught the bug. They began to cry and wouldn't suckle; their bottoms were sore and their tummies hard (all signs of tummy upset) – and they were only twenty-four hours old. The veterinary surgeon arrived and gave them (!) and mum injections and took a sample from a pup for analysis. The babies then had to be given 0.5 cc of medicine each twice a day for five days. I used a syringe with a small plastic tube attached. All except one were soon better: the odd one out deteriorated fast and had to be put to sleep. The bitch recovered quickly and her babies grew into lovely, healthy pups who never looked back.

The newly whelped bitch probably won't want any solid food for a couple of days but it does no harm to offer her a small dish of meat and tripe. If she eats it, she must be feeling well and can be given two meat meals per day. Until she takes solids give her plenty of milk and milky cereal with glucose, plus eggs. In the event of a large litter, she will need at least three pints of milk daily, gradually increasing towards weaning time (around three weeks) up to five pints. Her food should be divided into four good meals a day: two milk and cereal with egg, and two of meat with some meal. Plus a drink of milk at bed-time. Fresh water must always be available.

It is very important to continue her calcium and vitamin supplements during the next eight weeks or so, as she is under a great strain from feeding a large family. Most bitches do not like leaving their new litter even to eat so mine have their food in the box for a time. Their solid food intake is usually around 3–4 lb a day once over the first few days after whelping.

When the veterinary surgeon comes at four days to remove the puppies' dew claws someone she trusts should take mum for a walk on a lead for ten minutes so that she is not distressed by their cries. The vet should ensure that there is no bleeding and a clean sheet should be put in the box to protect against infection of the wounds. The puppies will cry a while but with their dam back they will soon be suckling again and her soothing tongue will comfort them. They do not normally cry for more than half an hour, if the job is done properly.

On the fifth day the dam might enjoy going for her usual walk. Certainly after a week she should – it is necessary for her health and helps milk production. Watch her closely though, she may suddenly have misgivings about her infants' welfare and shoot off home.

After each walk in the first week I always wash her undercarriage, hindquarters and feet with a weak solution of warm water and TCP to guard against infection. Dry her thoroughly before letting her in with the pups. When the puppies are two weeks old they are usually strong and healthy and full of mother's antibodies. Their nails should be cut every week as mum's teats take quite a pummelling at this time. Just trim off the little hook, it's quite easy. After the first week the temperature can be reduced gradually to 65°F. (18·3°C.), which will please mum.

If it is winter time and you move your litter from the house to an outside puppy kennel when they are around two to three weeks old, you must be very careful to avoid any sudden drop in room temperature. The bed in the puppy-house must be heated to at least 65°F. (18·3°C.) day and night. The dam should have a separate raised bed to enable her to escape the demands of her children when she wants to.

Puppies should be wormed at the earliest possible age, as they always seem to have some, and the longer it is left the more damage the worms will do. Ask your veterinary surgeon if there is a new worming drug available for puppies under three weeks. If there is nothing new, I have used St Aubrey Early Worm liquid with great success at three weeks old. They are dosed every seven to ten days after this until quite free. This is very important as bad worm infestation is deadly to young puppies. People who put off worming their puppies till five weeks are in danger of losing them. Coopane worm tablets are also excellent, if coated with butter.

With a large litter it is a good idea to begin teaching the puppies to eat and drink at about two weeks old. To begin with they will put more outside than inside but by three weeks they will be getting the message.

I usually start weaning with a teaspoon each of raw scraped skirt – human consumption beef. The best time is when mum is out for a walk and they are hungry.

I have a seat in the puppy-house, plus a large deep cardboard box lined with a soft blanket in which I pop the pups after feeding. It saves one ending up with a double quota. Mind you, when you have been handling them like this for a week, you can soon tell one from another. I put a towel on my lap, place a puppy on it, put a tiny piece of scraped meat on my finger and insert it about an inch into pup's mouth. As it suckles hopefully the meat will be swallowed. Sometimes they don't like the first taste and spit it out, so try again. Use scraped meat for the first week, gradually increasing the quantity as they accept it.

At this age I introduce them to Lactol, which is excellent for weaning pups. Obviously, this is given at a different time of day. This is a much more messy business and the towel needs to be around their fronts, as they get very sticky. I take a saucer and put a tablespoon of the warm mixture into it, gently dip in the pup's nose and let it lick its nose. With luck it will try to lick the saucer but often the whole business horrifies the puppy and it doesn't want to know. Each day they like it more and when they can all lap from a saucer try giving it in larger dishes on the floor. After each milky feed, it will be necessary to rinse off the milk stains with warm water and dry them thoroughly. If there is a chance of them getting a chill leave them sticky.

When they eat the scraped meat with ease, you can change to finely minced raw meat. Once all can eat and drink without help, the meals can be placed in several large dishes on the floor and pups placed around them. You must watch to make sure everyone gets a fair share. If they have reached this advanced stage at three weeks, they can be having two milky meals and one meat meal a day. Mum continues feeding them for another two or three weeks however.

When weaning, gradually increase the quantities as necessary. By four weeks I change the Lactol for a full cream dried milk powder. Glucose and Farlene, or similar, should be added to make the mixture creamy, thick and warm; feed twice a day plus meat twice a day. The minced meat can now be cooked (as it can now be a lower grade quality) and tripe added.

By five weeks, the puppies will have some form of meal or brown bread added to their meat meals, softened with stock or similar. Soft biscuits can accompany the two main milk meals and an extra small milk drink can be added at bedtime.

At four weeks old the puppies may start venturing outside in their run so as well as having newspaper on the kennel floor, put several double sheets down on the run floor – held down by weights at the corners – and they will start to housetrain themselves.

At six weeks the puppies should be completely independent of their dam for nourishment. Their meals should have been gradually increasing in size and they should be given as much at each meal as they will eat. Each puppy will be drinking about two-thirds of a pint of milky food per day and it is beneficial to add a raw egg, whisked in a little boiling water. The quantity of meat, etc. eaten by each puppy can vary but will probably be in the region of 6 ounces of meat plus meal. The vitamin and calcium additives given to the dam can also be fed to the puppies at this age, e.g. one calcium tablet, one Canovel and a drop of Adexolin per puppy. The food goes on increasing until it reaches the quantities shown in the Diet Sheet in Chapter 2.

The dam should continue to be given four meals a day up till the puppies are weaned and then her milk should be cut out. However, she needs lots of good food for some weeks ahead to build up her reserves. Weaning should be a natural process and mum should be allowed free access to the puppies during the day.

Once the puppies reach about four weeks, she will probably not want to sleep with them any more but will demand admission first thing in the morning. You will have to watch that she doesn't eat their food as she will if given the opportunity. From around four weeks onwards, she may regurgitate her food for her babies, as part of the natural weaning process. You will have to watch her and if she does, give her minced food only as large lumps can choke a puppy. It is really better all round if she doesn't bring up her food as she needs it more than her already well-fed puppies. It helps if she is kept away from them for an hour after her meals but this does not always stop her as it is a very strong instinct. She will probably help the puppies eat it up again but if she gives them a lot you must give her an extra helping afterwards to compensate.

It is worth re-emphasizing here one of the biggest dangers to a litter of healthy puppies – draughts and cold. The risk is obviously increased when the puppies are moved from the house to the puppy kennel. Their bed should be raised slightly and all low level cracks plugged. Keep a thermometer on the wall of the puppies box and be ready to provide extra heat (i.e. another infra red lamp or wall-hanging heaters) should the weather turn colder.

I have already warned against paraffin stoves but feel it is worth recalling a near-tragedy of my own.

Years ago I had a litter born at the end of January and they were in a puppy house in a brick room at the north-east of the house. The weather turned really cold so I supplemented the infra red lamp with a paraffin stove screwed to the floor at the opposite end of the room. I was slightly bothered about the fumes so I left a window slightly ajar. I kept a close eye on this arrangement and all seemed well when a friend baby-sat for me on the day of Cruft's show. Unfortunately it was during that day the weather really turned Arctic. A blizzard raged for hours and when we were allowed out of Olympia at 8 p.m. the roads were absolutely treacherous and even the North Circular was full of abandoned cars. The windscreen wipers kept icing up and we crawled home in four hours instead of the normal one.

It was a nightmare leading to another nightmare as we arrived to find the new litter were ill. The room contained only a little heat and a lot of fumes and the draught from the window was freezing.

Everything was quickly reorganized with electric heaters replacing the stove. But the pups developed pneumonia and twice a day for the next week the veterinary surgeon had to call to administer antibiotics and, as a different puppy reached a crisis, rush it to the surgery for oxygen. They were very ill and we were extremely lucky not to lose any. There were only five in the litter which was just as well in view of the individual nursing that was necessary. The only obvious effect was on one puppy who dragged a hind leg until he was eleven weeks old. The veterinery surgeon put this down to the large doses of antibiotics received at such a tender age.

However, it was an unlucky litter as three developed kidney failure or cancer by the age of seven. Whether some damage was done internally, by the illness and antibiotics, which did not develop until middle age, or it would have happened anyway, I don't know. In any case, I have never used a paraffin stove since.

Another puppy-time hazard is eclampsia in the dam. This can occur at any time during lactation but is most usual around two to three weeks when the puppies are growing and needing more and more nourishment and the bitch needs more and more good food and milk. If a big litter is not weaned early enough, the dam cannot cope and develops eclampsia. The signs to look for are glassy eyes, stiff, jerky movements, and if further advanced, the bitch can fall to the ground and have convulsions.

Any eclampsia is an emergency. Treatment by the veterinary surgeon consists of injecting a special calcium composition straight into the vein very slowly indeed – it can take twenty minutes as the veterinary surgeon watches the bitch for recovery symptoms and injects a little at a time. Eclampsia is quite frightening as it happens so quickly but with immediate expert treatment, it is soon over. However, puppies must be quickly weaned and the bitch kept away as much as possible, without upsetting her. It is essential to give a lactating bitch an adequate supply of balanced calcium and phosphorous, and Vitamin D, as stated earlier.

When puppies are six weeks old they should look really well – large, well boned babies with good bodies, healthy coats and shining eyes. If they don't, then something is wrong – perhaps they are not getting the correct quantity and quality of food, or they might still have worms and should be dosed again. Puppies sometimes go off their food and look a bit sorry for themselves without actually being ill and this could be a touch of tonsillitis.

Look down their throats, pressing down the tongue with your forefinger, and if you see small red tonsils then there is your problem. If you cannot see anything, then they are normal. Ask your veterinary surgeon to call and examine them, either way.

It is important to make a vermin check of the coats and skins of the dam and puppies, although it is unusual for puppies to carry lice or fleas. They could have been infected by mum. It is difficult to treat young puppies as many adult preparations are not suitable, and might be harmful. This is another case for your veterinary surgeon's advice.

Regular grooming and handling is essential for checking on other things than livestock. Puppies start to get used to handling when they are weaned and it is important to handle them gently and firmly, so they grow up confident and happy with people.

Take each one on to your lap every day from about four weeks old (time permitting) and gently groom them with a soft brush, talking quietly all the while. They soon become accustomed to the feel of the brush and the sound of your voice. I always rub their tummies, which they love, and when I put them to bed they soon start to roll on their backs expectantly.

From six weeks you can start to pose them on a steady table. Use a piece of rubber mat to stop them slipping and be very careful they don't spring off. You can also use the table top for grooming.

Classification into show quality and pets can begin at this stage. However, they change a little every week and be prepared to change your opinion more than once between six to ten weeks. The best time to choose the puppies for yourself and customers is between eight to eleven weeks. If possible get your bitch's breeder or the stud dog owner to come and give an opinion. The points of a potential show pup are covered in Chapter 2.

The most difficult part of breeding a litter is finding suitable homes for the puppies. If you are unknown in the show-ring it is even more difficult. For instance, if you were showing your bitch fairly successfully before breeding from her, other exhibitors would know you and be able to send along buyers. Otherwise, you start from scratch.

In the latter case, you inform the stud dog owner when the litter is born – how many, what sex etc. He may be able to send on inquiries. Also you can join the Dog Breeders Associates who will send you buyers (address: Mrs S. Blumire, 1 Abbey Road, Bourne End, Buckinghamshire, SL8 5NZ). Or the Kennel Club will forward inquiries if you have a registered prefix or affix and have advertised in the *Kennel Gazette*. If you are a member of any of the Irish Setter clubs (see Appendix B), you can inform the secretary of your litter.

Advertising is also recommended – local papers, dog papers, certain Sunday papers like the *Sunday Times*, and magazines like *The Lady* or *Horse and Hound*.

Any inquirers should be thoroughly vetted for suitability. Questions such as mentioned in Chapter 2 should be asked, e.g. Is there anyone at home during the day? Have you a fenced garden? etc.

Selling the puppies can be a relief after all those regular chores of cleaning up and feeding which seem to follow each other endlessly. It can also be heart-rending as the growing pups are very endearing. Your biggest responsibility is finding them good permanent homes.

Prospective buyers must be able to give the Setter the necessary time, attention and love – for possibly fifteen years. They will need to be at home to look after the puppy and must be made aware of exercising and feeding requirements of a boisterous, growing Irish Setter – also the not inconsiderable expense of keeping one.

Mistakes at this time could mean your beautifully reared puppy could be turned into an unhappy, unloved dog who is hungry, neglected and regarded as a nuisance. The Irish Setter Breeders Club has a hard-worked Rescue Scheme which can tell some horrifying stories of dogs no longer wanted.

Beware of the buyers who want a present for someone else, or for a too young child. A present of a lively puppy can soon become the last thing someone wants. Also, the mother of one or more very young children very rarely has the time, energy or affection left over for a puppy. It is far better to advise such a person to wait until the children are at least of school age before buying a dog. Otherwise the chances are that you will get a series of complaints about the puppy, leading up to the dog needing a new home any time from six months onwards.

Anyone breeding a litter should be responsible for the future welfare of each puppy and should make it a condition of sale to return the dog if the owner has to part with it for any unforeseen reason. If you are careful to vet each home (if possible go and see the family at home) this eventuality should not arise too often. However, it is far better to have the dog back and look at leisure for a more suitable home, than to hear that it has changed hands several times and has been put down or ended up in a dogs' home.

Don't dodge your responsibilities now. If you do, you are as bad as the 'puppy factories' that use such innocents to line their pockets.

When you get an inquiry ask some of the most important questions and if the answers are all right, suggest the family, especially mother, comes to see the dogs and have a chat. When they arrive, do not show them the puppies immediately but get them to sit down and bring in a few adult dogs to see how they react – you can glean a fair amount of information from this.

Give them a cuppa and get them to talk: ask the odd question, without weighting it either way so they give their own replies. They will reveal their attitudes to dogs and the reason why they want one. It might be a status symbol or perhaps a guard dog! Neither are good reasons and Irish Setters on the whole don't make good guards.

If they seem genuine people, who obviously love dogs but don't know much about them, then set about educating them. Tell them all about the breed: character, exercise, training, grooming, feeding etc., plus all the diabolical things they do while growing up. If they are still keen, show them the puppies and go on from there.

When you sell a puppy give a comprehensive diet/care sheet and go over it with the buyer before the puppy leaves for its new home. Also tell them about worming, grooming, travelling, and books which may be helpful, and any individual points concerning their puppy.

Buyers are delighted if you suggest keeping in touch to help sort out any little problems.

Puppy prices should be scaled from the best show prospect to the ones considered pets. No one can be quite sure how a puppy will finish up, no matter how beautiful it is at eight weeks, so never guarantee the buyer a certain champion. The best that can be said is 'most promising for show'. Never sell anything for show if it is not good enough; your reputation will stand or fall by your honesty. An exhibitor needs a high quality exhibit to win in the show-ring; anything less can involve fruitless time and expense and cause disappointment.

All your puppies must be in good health and condition when you sell them. It is as important for pet owners as for exhibitors to have a happy, healthy puppy. They need a signed pedigree, registration card and transfer form, plus the earlier-mentioned diet sheet. The puppies should not be sold before their eighth week.

If this is purely a 'one-off' litter you won't require your own registered affix but if this litter is the foundation of your own line, then you will need to apply to the Kennel Club some time before the pups are born for an application form for a registered affix of your own. The Kennel Club will require you to submit about six different made-up words for this purpose. As there are thousands of registered affixes, it is quite a job to hit on one that is original.

When you have your affix, or it is in the pipeline, you must decide what to call the pups, and your litter should then be registered at the Kennel Club. For this you need a KC blue Form 1. It must be signed by the stud dog owner at the time of mating with all necessary details completed.

You keep this form until after the litter is born in order to fill in your side with details of date of birth, number and sex of puppies.

You can register all or part of your litter, the fee for each puppy being £4·60. Any pups not named will receive a partly completed form from the KC which the future owner will be able to complete and send with fee, to the KC to register it themselves.

Exporting

When exporting a dog or puppy you must be even more careful about its intended home and environment. Once it has left this country, the six-month quarantine rule comes into force.

If it is possible for the buyer to come to England to choose the puppy and take it back with him, this is ideal. It is always more satisfactory to meet and talk with a possible buyer than to rely on letters or telephone communication. However, it is often not convenient for someone from overseas to make the journey. In this case, ask for details of their present dogs' routine, environment etc., and draw your own conclusions. If it is possible, try to get an informed independent opinion or reference.

The majority of overseas buyers who want show and breeding stock to improve their own strains are prepared to pay a fair price for a show quality animal and will mostly give it a good home. For your part, it is important to sell only top quality dogs abroad for show.

Some countries are not suitable for Irish, so be careful. There are various rules and regulations for each country importing dogs from Great Britain. If you are dealing with the actual export yourself, ask your veterinary surgeon for the details or contact the Ministry of Agriculture at Tolworth, Surrey. They are very helpful and will advise what papers and veterinary work is needed.

If you are sending the puppy by air, you will need a suitable box made by one of the shipping companies or airlines. There is a lot you will need to know before sending a puppy abroad. An experienced breeder would probably give you advice and the airlines are quite helpful. The puppy will need an Export Pedigree which the Kennel Club will supply on application with the appropriate fee.

If you prefer to employ an agent, make inquiries as to the best and most thorough. Although the easiest method of exporting, it is slightly more expensive.

5
The Show-ring

People become dog show enthusiasts either by accident or intention. In Chapter 2 I have described how the latter should go about obtaining a show pup. However, many people, myself included, started exhibiting by accident.

My own experience is typical. I fell in love with the first Irish Setter I came across. He was thirteen, greying, had hair sweeping the ground and was blind into the bargain – and I thought he was gorgeous. I made up my mind then and there that when I started to earn my own living I would save up and buy an Irish Setter. It was two years before the 'wherewithal' became available and then I had to find a breeder.

Being completely ignorant, I had no idea how to go about it but was lucky enough to obtain a three-month dog puppy through friends who knew some people who had English Setters, who knew someone with a litter of Irish Setters! This litter was bred by a complete novice and I was not given a diet sheet or any advice or instructions on how to bring him up. I had no idea how to go about it, so considering everything he turned out quite well.

I bought him purely for a companion and to me he was the most beautiful creature in the world. I had no idea that dog shows even existed – except, perhaps Cruft's – and would never have thought of showing him had not an established breeder seen him with me one day and suggested I entered him at a small local show as he was quite nice. I was in two minds as I didn't know what I was letting myself in for.

However, at the last moment I did enter and duly presented seven-month-old Pluto at our first dog show. I was lucky it was a famous gundog judge who was very kind to a completely clueless novice and Pluto ended up with a second prize. Of course, that was it – I was well and truly bitten by the bug. After that, I read every book on dogs at the local library, bought or borrowed many more and slowly began to realize that I was doing everything wrong!

However, that's another story. What happened to me has happened countless other times to other people and will doubtless go on *ad infinitum*.

It is obviously far more sensible to start your show career with a properly schooled dog and handler. This can be accomplished at your local canine society's ring training classes. Such societies usually run monthly match meetings as well. These are excellent events for introducing young puppies (six months onwards) to other dogs and to showing. In fact, it is a good idea to take a puppy to training classes and matches from about four months old, just to sit and watch and absorb the atmosphere, noises, people and strange dogs. By the time he is six months old it will all seem quite normal and nothing to worry about.

However, you must be careful to watch that nothing happens to frighten the puppy. If he gets bitten or roughly handled he will associate it with the show environment and be nervous and jumpy at shows. At a good ring training class the handler will be coached as well as the dog. Of course, trainers won't be conversant with all the many different methods of handling various breeds but this is something you can pick up by attending a few shows by yourself.

Show training really starts when your puppy is about eight weeks and is even then getting used to being handled. Place him on a steady table with a non-slip surface and gently groom him, talking softly all the while to promote confidence. After grooming, go through a quick routine of looking at teeth and standing him in a show pose for a few seconds. Follow this with praise, general fuss and a tit-bit. Repeat the training – and rewards – several times a week but for short periods only. As he gets older and bigger it is more convenient to use an oblong bench, about eighteen inches high, which he will soon jump on to in anticipation of grooming, attention and tit-bits.

Taking him for walks is the best way to accustom him to the collar and lead and will pave the way for training on a show-lead. Arm yourself with a favourite tit-bit and take him to a spot where you can run him up and down and in a triangle. When you begin, take it steady otherwise he will get over-excited and leap up.

Follow the trial run and tit-bit with a few seconds in a show pose. Do this a couple of times and then call it a day. Never overdo the training or he will get bored and naughty. If when you are practising someone acts as the judge, so much the better. A gentle look at the teeth and some handling will prepare him for future ring procedure.

A word of warning: if he is misbehaving, and you can feel yourself becoming angry, stop at once and try again the following day. If you lose your temper you are likely to upset him and put him off showing for good. A dog must enjoy showing – a miserable dog looks awful.

The next step is getting the puppy used to strange places full of noisy human beings. Apart from the show training classes and matches, it helps to take him to the local, but be careful he is not given too much to drink! People always want to make a fuss of puppies and stroke them, and this is all to the good. They thoroughly enjoy the attention.

Another important point is travelling to shows. People mostly travel by car or coach nowadays so your Setter must learn to travel happily. I have mentioned in a previous chapter that the best way to tackle this problem is psychologically. Irish Setters adore their gallops so if you use a car to get to the exercise area he will soon build up pleasurable walkie associations with the car.

On a long journey, at the beginning of a puppy's show career, I give him one or two Sealegs travel sickness pills (they are made for people); perhaps one the night before and one about two hours before the journey. These are the best pills for travel sickness that I've tried. As the puppy gets used to long journeys I give him just one pill the night before. Afterwards, I try without any and usually he is fine. Veterinary surgeons tend to prescribe tranquillizers for travel sickness. The dose is given about an hour before the journey and by the time you arrive at the show, the puppy is half drugged with sagging red eyes. It takes all day to recover and looks appalling. You certainly cannot show a dog in this condition.

As your puppy grows up and starts to look a little more like an Irish Setter, and less like a young colt with a whippety tail, you can think about entering for a show. The best way to see how he is looking (from a judge's viewpoint) is to stand him in front of a mirror, a large one of course. You can see if he looks old enough or is standing correctly. It is an excellent way of improving your handling. For instance, is his head and neck at the right angle? Are his stifles correctly bent? Be sure his front legs are straight underneath him and his feet are neither turned out nor in. You can learn the correct stance by watching the seasoned exhibitors at shows.

Shows are advertised in the two-weekly dog papers, *Our Dogs* and *Dog World*. The entries usually close between three to six weeks before the show day. Write to the secretaries for a schedule.

Before entering, you must check that the dog is registered with the Kennel Club in your name. If not, as long as you send the registration off, with appropriate fee, you can still enter the show with the chosen name followed by NAF (name applied for). If it is the transfer to your ownership that is still in the pipeline, the same rule applies and you follow the dog's name with TAF (transfer applied for).

There is a small type of show where any dog is eligible as they do not have to be registered at the Kennel Club. This is an Exemption Show which includes novelty classes open to all dogs however they are bred. There are four classes for pedigree dogs only and eight novelty classes for all. These shows are usually in conjunction with village fêtes, horse shows etc., and charity events. They are quite useful for giving a puppy experience but are not intended for serious dog show exhibitors – rather for the family pet.

The pedigree dog shows are divided into four categories:

Sanction Show: this is a small affair limited to members of the organizing canine society (membership can be applied for with entries). Usually twenty classes or less, for dogs which have not won five or more first prizes in post graduate classes etc. Challenge certificate winners are ineligible.

Limited Show: a slightly bigger show, again for club members. CC winners cannot enter.

Open Show: open to all comers under Kennel Club rules, including CC winners and champions. More likely to have breed classes with a specialist judge. There are also Any Variety classes under an all-rounder who judges many different breeds. Large Open Shows are often benched, i.e. a benched compartment for each exhibit when not being judged or exercised. This show schedules anything from fifty classes upwards.

Championship Show: this type of show is also open to all, with the exception of Cruft's for which exhibits have to qualify. It schedules many different breeds, most of which have Kennel Club challenge certificates on offer for the best dog and bitch in each breed. Three challenge certificates, awarded by three different judges, entitle a dog or bitch to be called a champion or, in the case of an Irish Setter, a show champion. Gundogs have to qualify in the field to gain the full champion title. Championship shows are also benched.

There are at least thirty general championship shows each year in Great Britain, plus Breed Club specialist championship events for most breeds. The Irish Setter Association of England, the Irish Setter Breeders Club and the Irish Setter Club of Scotland each stage an annual championship show, while others of special interest to the 'Irish' fraternity are the championship shows of the Setter and Pointer Club and the National Gundog Association.

Kennel Club titles and awards:

Champion –	a winner of three challenge certificates under three different judges, plus a field trial award for gundogs.
Show Champion –	as above, for gundogs only, without the field trial award.
Junior Warrant –	This is awarded to a dog gaining twenty-five points before he is eighteen months old. Points come from first prizes won in breed classes at only Open and Championship Shows: one point for a first at Open Shows, and three points for a Championship Show first.

It is always pleasant to win a Junior Warrant with one's young hopeful, as it proves he is promising but it is not as important – or as elevating – as a challenge certificate. Often one's first CC comes unexpectedly and it is a very heady experience – quite marvellous.

Cruft's Dog Show merits a special mention, as it is run by the dog world's ruling body, the Kennel Club, and a dog needs to qualify in order to enter. This most famous of all championship shows is always held in February and is the first general championship show of the new year. To qualify, it is necessary to win a particular prize at a championship show during the previous year, as laid down by the Cruft's Dog Show Committee. Dog show enthusiasts greatly prize such a win as there is obvious kudos in showing at Cruft's – the best known event in dogdom. Quite often advertisements appear in the dog papers saying so-and-so has 'qualified for Cruft's'. For this show certainly has a magic of its own and there are very few exhibitors who care to miss it. Organized parties and individuals come from all over the world and in our breed the open classes frequently attract the year's biggest gathering of Show Champions. Unlike their 'lesser' fellows, Show Champions do not have to qualify for Cruft's.

The magic of Cruft's has also gained it a rare honour – a place on British television. Filming often takes place while judging is in process and is shown (oh, so briefly) the Sunday following. It is a great pity that dog shows receive such sparse coverage by the media as dog showing is a very popular sport and deserves promoting just as much as greyhound racing or showjumping.

But to get back to your youngster and his show début. If you have done your initial training at your local club matches etc., and the puppy is behaving quite reasonably, I would suggest you enter a breed class at an Open Show.

You may think that perhaps a Sanction or Limited would be enough for a start but these events rarely schedule breed classes. Also they often take place in small, crowded halls where there is nowhere for your dog to relax. People and other dogs will always be stepping on or over him, and perhaps because of the congestion, another dog might growl or snap at him, and this could upset or put him off.

The majority of Open Shows, particularly the summer outdoor events are not so congested because they are bigger and there is more room. Usually there are several rings with different breeds being judged concurrently. If benching is not available, there should be plenty of room to sit with your dog around the breed ring and watch the judging. There is often something to be learned this way.

The entry form in the show schedule should be completed and sent off with accompanying fee, before the entries close. Completing the form is quite simple as all the details and information are either in the schedule or on the entry form. Your puppy's particulars are on his registration card. The classes are listed in the schedule and the definition of each class appears towards the front. Read the information in the schedule very carefully and check your entry before posting. One or two classes is enough at this stage, otherwise he will soon get bored and start playing up.

Once your entry has been accepted, you should check that your dog is in show condition, which really means that he should be in general good health. If he is fit and well, properly fed and exercised, he will look good, and attention to coat and nails adds just the finishing touch.

I have already discussed grooming in the chapter on growing-up. If you groom your setter regularly, he should have a shining, well-kept coat. Keep his nails short. Frequent shampooing is not necessary, unless he has rolled in something nasty or got himself really dirty. When they are changing coats, a good bath helps to remove all the old, loose hair. Use a good shampoo – human or canine – and wash and rinse twice, then finish off with conditioner, rinse and dry thoroughly with towels. If he is going to a show, it helps if you finish off with a hand dryer and brush. It is probably better to carry out the washing two or three days before the show. However, it is not a good idea to wash him very often as this removes the coat's natural oils and in any case Irish have naturally lovely silky and shining coats.

Try to get your dog's body-weight just right – neither thin nor fat but with his ribs and haunch bones covered and a slight waist at the loin.

Trimming is something you learn from other people; if it is done incorrectly your Setter can look awful for weeks. A friendly breeder or exhibitor will probably show you what to do and you can pick up the finer points as you go to more shows. Luckily, a Setter puppy doesn't usually need a lot of trimming as the feathering is only just beginning to grow. Of course, ears can appear rather bushy with the mixture of old baby hair and new adult growth but these should be trimmed by an expert with you watching and learning. The front of the neck and the feet need some attention too. Never take your show dog to a canine beauty parlour – few professional dog trimmers have ever prepared an Irish Setter for show. Electric clippers make short work of the beautiful chestnut top coat and expose the dull orange undercoat. Ugh!

Trimming tools that you will need are: a quite expensive pair of trimming scissors, a pair of good hair-cutting scissors, a stripping knife and a comb. Thinning scissors, and/or a knife, are used on ears, although some experts can achieve a beautiful effect with finger and thumb plucking. The feathering on the underside of the neck often needs some thinning out but never touch the hair on the back of the neck. Feet can be improved by trimming the perimeter with the sharp scissors. Excessive hair between the toes needs a little thinning out but leave a bit, otherwise you will get a slack, splay toed appearance.

The day before the show your youngster should be looking well, ready for the great day. You will need to pack a show bag.

The dog will require: a newspaper for the bench and a rug to go on top, benching chain (you can buy one at a show) and collar; water bowl; grooming equipment; tit-bits; towel; show-lead (also on sale at big shows) preferably a thin brown one, which will not spoil the outline of the neck; a dog chew, to help relieve boredom; special pin for holding your ring number (a safety pin is just as good). When I am showing a puppy, I often take along its lunch as it can be a long day.

You will need: a flask, bottle of milk (a little for your tea, a lot for the dog); sandwiches; schedule; exhibitor's pass and car park ticket. If it is an outdoor show be wise and pack Wellingtons, a mac and umbrella. Dog shows seem to get muddy at the slightest suspicion of rain, so wear warm, comfortable clothes rather than something for appearance sake.

On the morning of the show, give yourself plenty of time to exercise your dog before leaving and get to the show about an hour before judging commences. Allow for traffic hold-ups. It's disastrous to arrive late and have to dash straight into the ring, or find you have missed your class. Stress situations will add to the puppy's new ordeal so, for everyone's sake, have enough time in hand for a run in a nearby field, a drink (for the dog!) and the opportunity of taking stock of the strange goings-on. Remember, judging starts with the puppy classes so you could be in the ring as soon as the show starts.

If the show is benched, your pass will bear your benching number which can be confirmed by a quick glance at the catalogue, purchased close to the entrance with acrobatic agility, while holding an unsettled puppy, a show-bag, hand-bag, and still having a hand free to find the necessary money.

Find your bench and use it as a depository: your Setter on it and your bags underneath it. If it is puppy's first meeting with a show bench, reassurance and vigilance are necessary for quite some time. All too often one sees an unattended puppy tumble backwards off the front of the bench while tethered to the back. It is a very frightening experience and could be dangerous. So stay close until he is quite used to it – which might take several shows.

Once he realizes it is a safe bed to sleep on between showing and exercising (and mum does come back to sit with him and hasn't left him for ever!) a Setter is quite content to stay put. There was an occasion when I was showing two different breeds and, having finished showing one of my Irish, rushed her into the marquee and sped off to take a beagle into a class which had started. An hour later I popped back and she was fast asleep on her bench – completely unfastened. Of course, she was a show veteran and knew the ropes, but I was very lucky.

It is a good plan to take a companion to shows for a variety of reasons, not least the opportunity of splitting the 'puppy watch'.

Having sorted yourself out at the bench, check on the time of judging and the location of the relevant ring. You have still got to have a cuppa and then get puppy off the bench to groom him. About ten minutes before your class, take him to the ring to get him accustomed to the show atmosphere.

When the steward calls your class, take the puppy in, collect your ring number and try to stand near the end of the line of exhibits, so that you can check the judge's procedure and also allow the puppy time to settle down. If it is a big class take along a dog chew and some tit-bits; this will help to keep him amused although you may find he is more interested in playing with his neighbour.

Keep your eye on the judge and learn his routine so that when your turn arrives you won't become flustered. He will probably call a dog into the centre of the ring to stand in a show pose, inspect the front teeth, head and expression, run his hands over the body and legs, then stand back and view the exhibit before testing its movement. The movement exercise will usually involve the handler taking the dog at a trot in a straight line away and to the judge, and/or in a triangle.

When the judge has moved the final dog, all the exhibitors place the dogs in the show pose and the judge will walk round the ring picking out half a dozen or so from whom he will select his winners. The unselected leave the ring while the remaining ones may be required to 'stand' and 'move' until the judge decides the order of merit.

Whether you get placed or not, make a fuss of your puppy and he will remember showing with pleasure. Exercise him, if required, and take him back to his bench. You may be showing him in another class so keep an eye on how the judging progresses.

The rest of the day, until it is time to go home, can be spent looking after both yourself and your Setter, getting to know other exhibitors and – providing everything is all right at the bench – watching the judging. Dog show folk can be very nice and helpful but don't bother anyone when they are preparing for their classes, wait until afterwards.

You will find that among many people there are many opinions. They can't all be right, so take criticisms, advice, gossip etc. with a pinch of salt. When you have been around a little longer you can form your own opinions.

Occasionally, you will have someone give you an unsolicited opinion of your Setter, which may or may not be very nice. Don't get upset, it may have been said out of jealousy or ignorance. I doubt whether I would have been showing today if I had paid heed to the words of a renowned Setter person. That he considered my foundation dog unfit to be shown or bred from was very painful – but I think I had the last laugh.

In any case, there is – and always has been – a tremendous amount of goodwill among the Irish enthusiasts (maybe we take after our dogs).

If your puppy was not among the winners, it is quite in order, once judging has finished, to take him to the judge and ask where he failed against the others. Don't be surprised if you have to wait a few moments though, there are often many people wanting a word with the judge.

Showing dogs is a sport and it would be a good thing if everyone were to remember this. It's not a matter of life or death whether you win or lose, just the luck of the game. You can win a first, even a CC, one week, and the next, under another judge, not be placed at all! Judging is all a matter of opinion (always within the breed standard, of course) and opinions vary widely, which is why the same dog doesn't win every week – which I had such a hard job explaining to my father-in-law.

Sometimes a breed produces an outstanding dog or bitch

which has a run of top wins. This has happened in Irish Setters many times in the past. However, in the normal way at the championship shows there are several of each sex which are of high enough merit to win challenge certificates and will change places at different shows, depending on the judges' opinions, plus the individual animal's coat, condition, showmanship, movement etc. on the actual day.

Club championship shows and Cruft's usually attract the biggest entry of top class animals in the higher classes as exhibitors will make a greater effort to attend the special shows. The club championship shows often put on more classes and have club trophies and special prizes. In addition, you meet all your friends and have a jolly good – and exhausting – time.

The general championship shows have many trade stands where you can buy just about everything you can think of for your dogs. The variety of grooming equipment, lotions, conditioners, dog-coats, vitamin supplements, and dog foods of all sorts is most confusing. Dog books, herbal conditioners, insurance, beauty parlour equipment, special notepaper and cards etc. etc., it's incredible.

There are a number of winter shows, but the main show season is in the summer. General championship shows are so enormous with entries from 10000 to 18000 depending upon their popularity and accessibility. You can imagine the extra difficulty of trying to stage such an event indoors. It is so much easier to use a large open space, and have marquees for benching halls and wet weather accommodation. Parking is so much easier than in a city centre and the dogs enjoy the fresh air and exercise and usually show much better. Seeing some of them lifting their noses to the breeze – regardless of judge and spectators – makes one realize what a magnificent breed it is.

6

The Breed Standard

The original description of the breed was drawn up in 1886 by a group of Irish Setter owners in Ireland who founded a club named the Irish Red Setter Club, Dublin. In 1930 this standard was revised in Dublin and when the British Kennel Club later decided to bring all breed standards under their control, the revised Dublin standard was accepted as the official description of the breed with the exception of the Scale of Points which was deleted.

It is rather a sparse description in places compared to the standards of many other breeds, sparing in both words and explicit dimensions. This leaves the way open to differing types of Irish Setters being bred within the framework of the breed standard.

Kennel Club Breed Standard

Reproduced by permission of the Kennel Club.

General appearance. Must be racy, full of quality, and kindly in expression.

Head and skull. The head should be long and lean, not narrow or snipy, and not coarse at the ears. The skull oval (from ear to ear), having plenty of brain room, and with well-defined occipital protuberance. Brows raised, showing stop. The muzzle moderately deep, and fairly square at end. From the stop to the point of the nose should be long, the nostrils wide, and the jaws of nearly equal length, flews not to be pendulous. The colour of the nose, dark mahogany, or dark walnut, or black.

Eyes. Should be dark hazel or dark brown and ought not to be too large.

Ears. The ears should be of moderate size, fine in texture, set on low, well back; and hanging in a neat fold close to the head.

L to R: Sh. Ch. Joanma's Lottie (with her owner, Mrs. S. Culpin), and Sh. Chs. Cornevon Prince Charming and Cornevon Cinderella (with their owner, the author). All three are by Wendover Game. (*Alan J. Millard*)

'he famous 'T' litter. *L to R*: Sh. Chs. Twoacres Troilus, Twoacres Teresa, 'woacres Traviata and Twoacres Tamburlaine (*Percy Clegg*)

Sh. Ch. Wendover Happy-Go-Lucky (*Julian Kennedy-Sloane*)

Sh. Ch. Wendover Colas. Dog CC Cruft's 1977 (*Bob Heron*)

Sh. Ch. Joanma's Scampi. Bitch CC and B.O.B. Cruft's 1977

Sh. Ch. Cornevon Stargem. CC and B.O.B. Cruft's 1976 (*Michael Oakley*)

BELOW LEFT:
Cornevon Starbright (*Michael Oakley*)

Sh. Ch. Cornevon Lovebird. Dog CC Cruft's 1974, Irish Setter of the Year 1974 (*Michael Oakley*)

Hartsbourne Galanthus

Sh. Ch. Moyna Michelle (*Michael Oakley*)

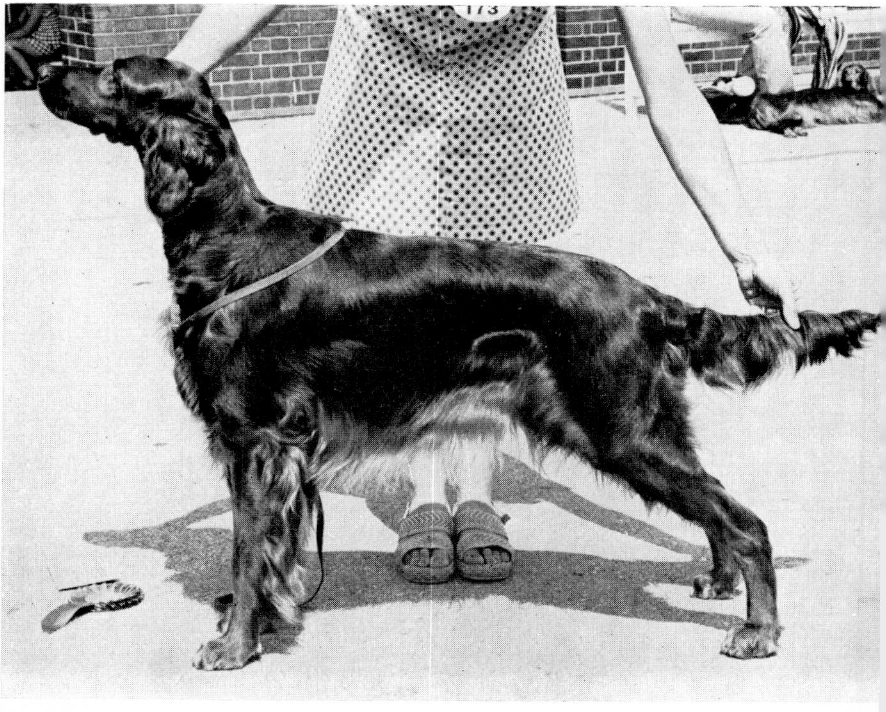

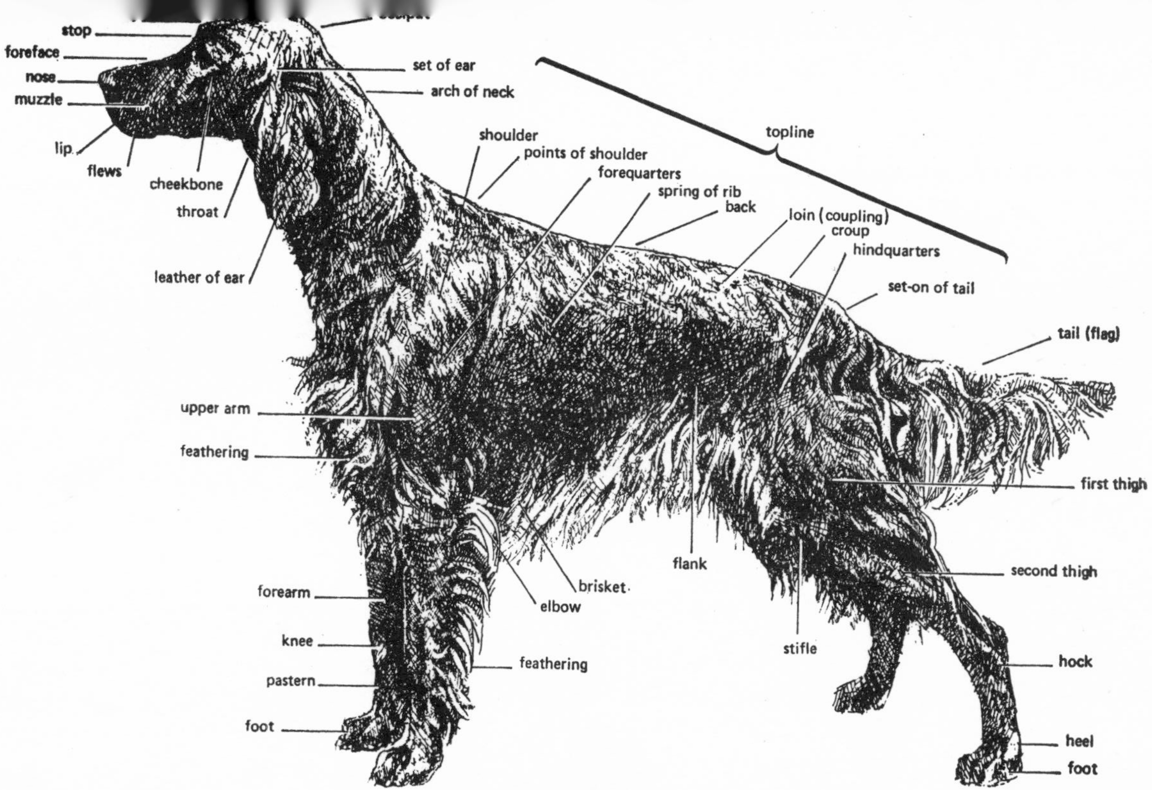
stop
foreface
nose
muzzle
lip
flews
cheekbone
throat
leather of ear
set of ear
arch of neck
shoulder
points of shoulder
forequarters
spring of rib
back
topline
loin (coupling)
croup
hindquarters
set-on of tail
tail (flag)
first thigh
second thigh
hock
heel
foot
stifle
flank
brisket
elbow
feathering
upper arm
feathering
forearm
knee
pastern
foot

Fig. 2 The points

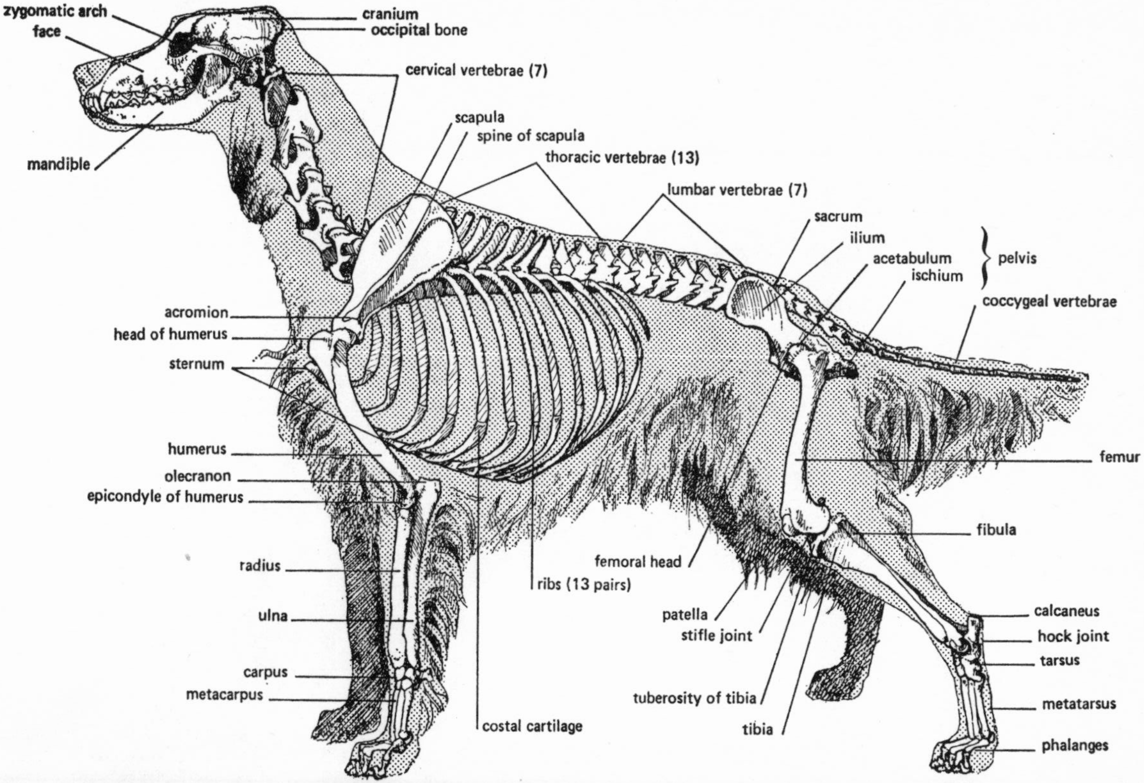
zygomatic arch
face
mandible
cranium
occipital bone
cervical vertebrae (7)
scapula
spine of scapula
thoracic vertebrae (13)
lumbar vertebrae (7)
sacrum
ilium
acetabulum
ischium
pelvis
coccygeal vertebrae
acromion
head of humerus
sternum
humerus
olecranon
epicondyle of humerus
radius
ulna
carpus
metacarpus
costal cartilage
ribs (13 pairs)
femoral head
patella
stifle joint
tuberosity of tibia
tibia
femur
fibula
calcaneus
hock joint
tarsus
metatarsus
phalanges

Mouth. Not over- or undershot.
Neck. Should be moderately long, very muscular, but not too thick, slightly arched, free from all tendency to throatiness.
Forequarters. The shoulders to be fine at the points, deep and sloping well back. The chest as deep as possible, rather narrow in front. The fore legs should be straight and sinewy, having plenty of bone, with elbows free, well let down, not inclined either in or out.
Body. Should be proportionate, the ribs well sprung, leaving plenty of lung room. Loins muscular, slightly arched.
Hindquarters. Should be wide and powerful. The hind legs from hip to hock should be long and muscular; from hock to heel short and strong. The stifle and hock joints well bent, and not inclined either in or out.
Feet. Should be small, very firm, toes strong, close together and arched.
Tail. Should be of moderate length, proportionate to the size of the body, set on rather low, strong at root, and tapering to a fine point; to be carried as nearly as possible on a level with or below the back.
Coat and feathering. On the head, front of the legs, and tips of the ears, should be short and fine, but on all other parts of the body and legs it ought to be of moderate length, flat, and as free as possible from curl or wave. The feather on the upper portion of the ears should be long and silky; on the back of fore and hind legs should be long and fine; a fair amount of hair on the belly, forming a nice fringe, which may extend on chest and throat. Feet to be well feathered between the toes. Tail to have a nice fringe of moderately long hair, decreasing in length as it approaches the point. All feathering to be as straight and flat as possible.
Colour. The colour should be rich chestnut, with no trace whatever of black; white on chest, throat, chin or toes, or a small star on the forehead, or a narrow streak or blaze on the nose or face not to disqualify.

Note: Male animals should have two apparently normal testicles fully descended into the scrotum.

Some notes on the standard

General appearance. This is well phrased and indicates a slim, elegant animal, with an air of royalty about it, who nevertheless has a muscular and powerful body built into a racy frame. The expression is a sweet one, conveying a kindly disposition and good humour.

Head and skull. From the side view, the head should give the appearance of two rectangular boxes divided by the stop into the upper (skull) and lower (muzzle) box. The head should never be coarse or heavy; the skull being oval from ear to ear but not broad or flat. The back of the slightly domed skull has the well defined occipital protuberance and the forehead is raised at the brows to show a defined stop. The cheek bones should be as flat as possible as rounded cheeks give a heavy coarse effect and detract from the desired long, lean head. The muzzle should be moderately deep but not as deep as the English or the Gordon, with a fairly

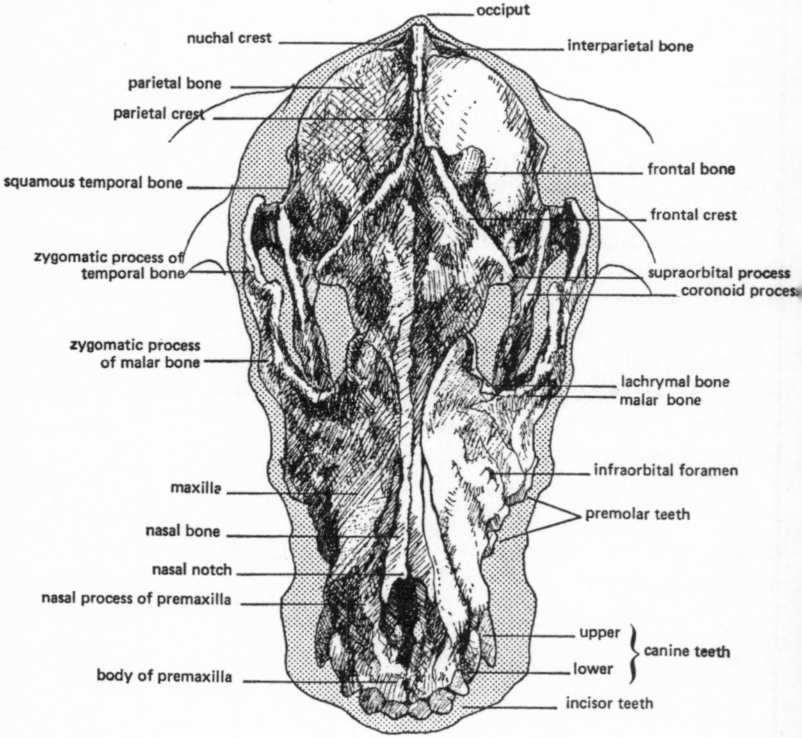

Fig. 4a The skull: front view

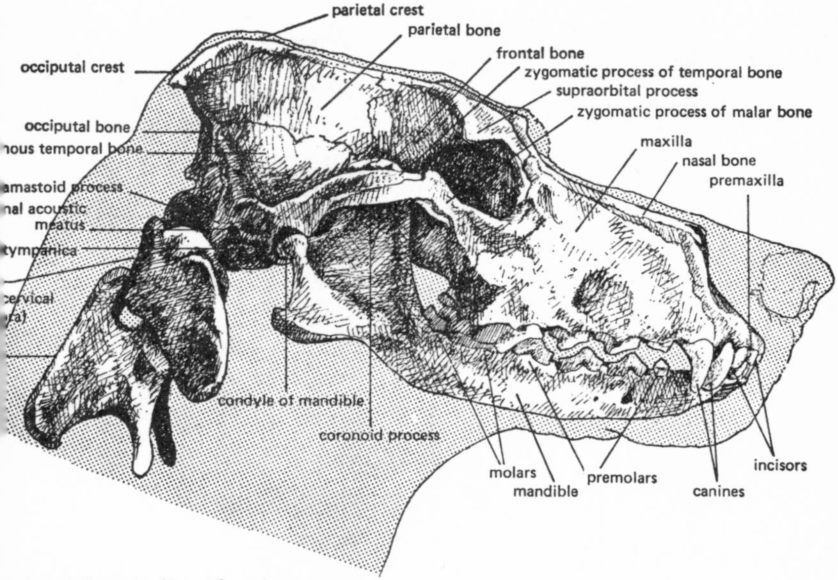

4b The skull: side view

square finish but never pointed or snipy. From the front, the muzzle should appear to be of sufficient breadth without being either too narrow or too broad, thereby losing the special Irish characteristic balance of head. The lips should cover the lower jaw but not be exaggerated in flew; viewed from the front, the chin should be visible. The nose fairly large with wide nostrils, the colour is clearly defined in the standard. The skull and fore-face should always be on parallel lines and deviations such as Roman-nose or dish-faced or a skull that inclines downwards towards the occipit are untypical and wrong. Equally wrong is a square heavy head with a deep stop and high set ears, or a too-fine, snipy head with no stop and a greyhoundy appearance.

Eyes. Should be of medium size, of a rather 'full' almond shape, but not Oriental, as this tends to harden the expression which should be soft, kindly and rather quizzical. The colour varies from dark brown to dark hazel. A light eye spoils the expression and a large round yellow eye is objectionable.

Ears. This paragraph is self-explanatory, but I will add that the shape of the ear is long and narrow, with an oval tip; if you

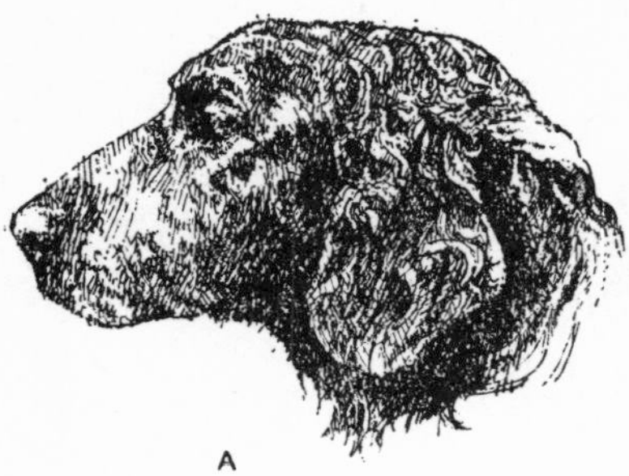

A

B

C

D

E

F

measure an adult's ear to the end of its nose, the ear will not quite reach to the end, perhaps three-quarters of an inch short of it. The texture of the ear should never be thick, and the set-on should be at, or below, eye level.

Mouth. 'Not over- or undershot.' This means a 'scissor' bite in which the top front teeth close smoothly over the bottom front teeth. An over-shot mouth is when the top front teeth project over the bottom ones, leaving a gap in between; an under-shot mouth is when the bottom front teeth stick out in front of the top front teeth. Both are serious faults.

Neck. A fairly long neck in proportion to the dog as a whole, gives the look of elegance and quality when it is combined with a graceful arch where the neck joins the head. Throatiness, or dewlap, appears as excessive folds of skin under the throat and is unsightly and undesirable.

Forequarters. A well laid-back shoulder, combined with a correctly angulated (rearwards) upper arm, should put the elbows almost in line with the points of the shoulder above. The arched neck should then blend into the shoulder blades with no ugly hump on the fine points of the shoulders. The deep chest reaches to the elbows or just below, and appears rather narrow from the front, when the dog is standing, but when sitting, the chest looks much wider and stronger. The forelegs should be quite straight and sinewy, with plenty of bone and strong, straight pasterns; elbows should not stick out or be tucked in, but free. Either of these positions produce bad, untypical movement.

Body. The length of body should be in proportion to the height of the dog, thus giving a well balanced appearance. The top-line

---

Fig. 5 Heads:

A. Incorrect non-parallel lines of skull and foreface, giving a downface appearance to muzzle and a backward slope of skull from brow to occiput; small, short ears.
B. Snipy muzzle, lacks stop, throaty; possibly overshot.
C. Short, squarish heavy head; broad skull; slightly dish-faced; not typical.
D. Correct head in profile.
E. Not typical; large, round light eyes, with hard, staring expression; coarse, projecting cheek-bones; ears' set-on wrong; triangular shape head.
F. Correct head, front view.

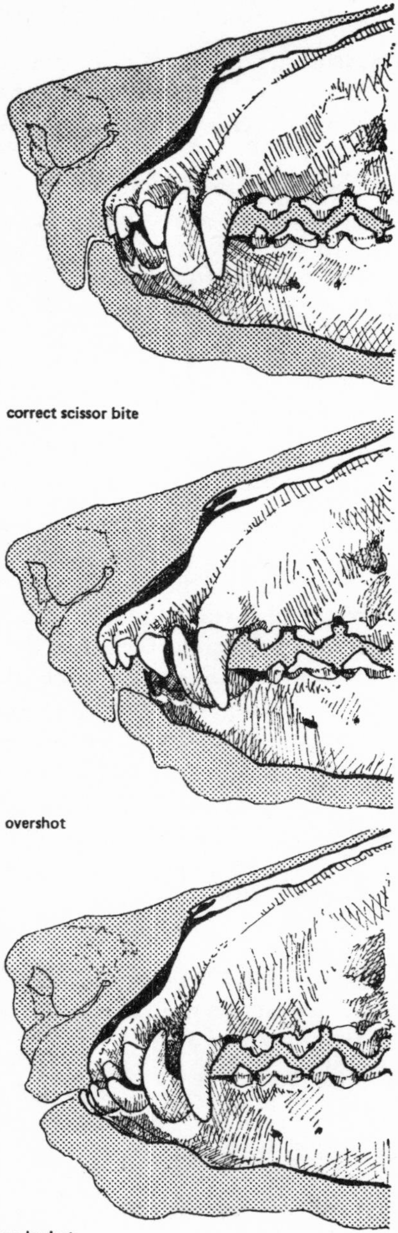

Fig. 6 The bite

A

B

Fig. 7 Faults:

A. Upright in shoulder; upward displacement of the vertebra at the dorsal/lumbar junction; roach back; projecting hips; weak hindquarters and straight stifles; weak pasterns; flat feet.

B. Unbalanced; Heavy in head for body, back too short; exaggerated slope to top-line; very weak hindquarters, not matching up to forequarters.

A

B

Fig. 8 Faults:

A. Sway-back; ewe-neck. Flat feet. 'Goose-rump' croup.

B. Faulty shoulder, neck set in slightly below points of shoulder blades, giving 'dowager's hump' or 'horse collar' effect. Steep croup.

A

B

Fig. 9 Faults:

A. Unbalanced: incorrect, level topline; too long in body and loin; over-angulated shoulder and fore-arm; short in leg; high tail-set.

B. Too long in loin; exaggerated bend of stifle, weak hocks placed too far behind body, probably giving 'wobbly' hind movement.

should have a gentle slope from the withers to the tail set-on; a dip behind the shoulder, sway back, or roach back are all wrong. The ribs should be well-sprung, but not barrel-ribbed or the opposite slab-sided; the ribs should extend well back. The loin should be strong, muscular and slightly arched with no tendency towards a weak, tucked-up look.

Hindquarters. The hindquarters are strong and powerful, the croup having a gentle slope to the set-on of tail. The hind legs from hip to hock being long and muscular to promote a well-bent stifle; the upper thigh to be broad and strong and the second thigh well developed; from hock to heel short, straight and strong. There should be no tendency towards cowhocks or toeing in.

Feet. Should be small, compact with strong, well-arched toes close together; pads are thick and well cushioned.

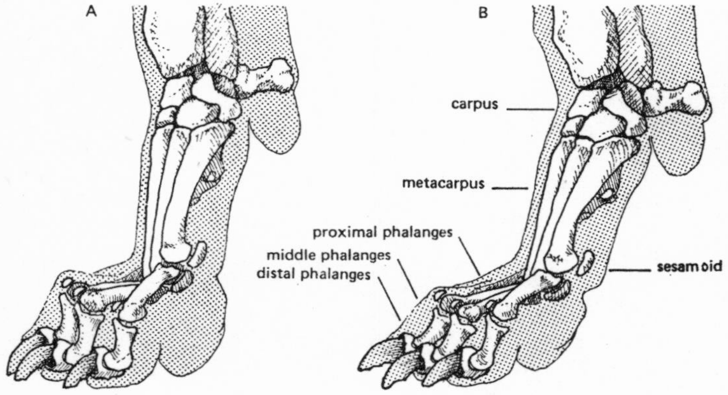

Fig. 10 Feet
A. Correct tight foot, toes arched.
B. Toes splayed, pasterns weak.

Tail. Length is in proportion to the rest of the dog; set-on just below the level of the back, thick at the root and tapering to a fine point, carried level with or below the back. When a Setter is standing still, if the point of the tail just touches the hock-joint, that should be the correct length.

Coat and feathering. The standard description is straightforward and easy to understand. However, one sees many different types of coat, ranging from Pointer coat, which is short, straight hair with no feathers, through to really curly, bushy coats – both of which are incorrect. A good coat has a lovely silky feel to it, and the feathers are fine and flat.

Colour. This is perhaps the most beautiful point of the Irish Setter. There is no other breed with the beautiful shining, deep chestnut colour coat. It can only be enhanced by the small flashes of white which the standard allows. The most common white marking to be seen in present times is a small white star or patch on the chest, throat or chin. Occasionally one sees a small white flash on the skull which is very attractive but often this disappears as a puppy grows up, as does the white on the toes. A blaze or streak on the nose is very rare in England, at least.

Character. The standard doesn't mention character, but this is just as important as conformation. The Irish Setter is basically a

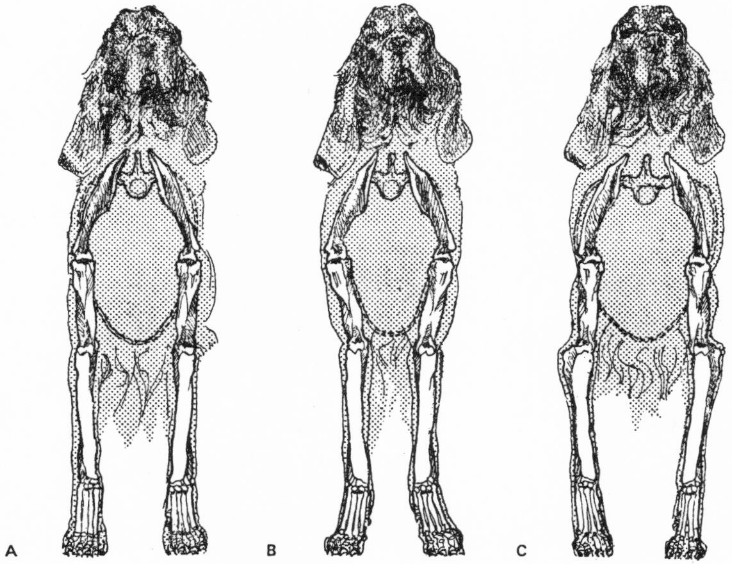

Fig. 11 Fronts, shoulders and ribs

A. Correct straight front, shoulders fine at the points, ribs well sprung
B. Elbows tucked in; associated with narrow rib-cage, and feet turning out.
C. Out at elbow; sometimes associated with barrel ribs (exaggerated spring) and feet turning in (pigeon-toed).

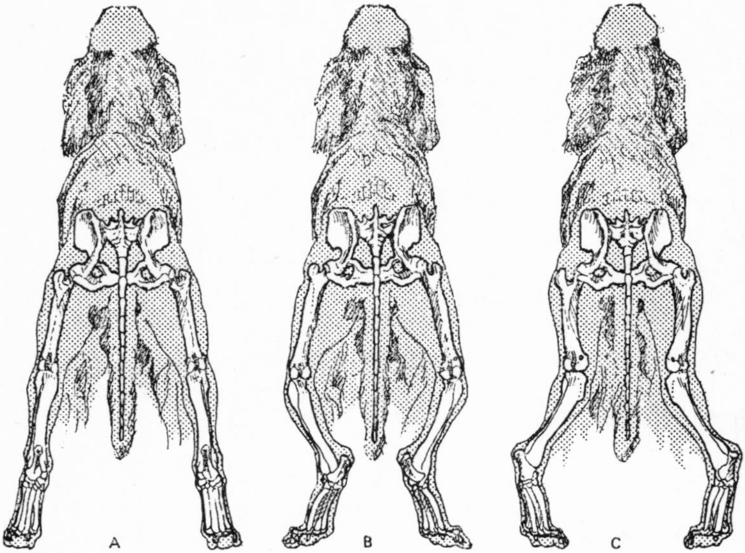

Fig. 12 Back views
A. Correct
B. Cow-hocked, with splayed feet.
C. Stifles turning in, hocks out, toes in.

gay, happy-go-lucky character, who loves his family and his friends, both human and canine. When young, he is boisterous and carefree; likes nothing better than a romp or gallop with other youngsters – again both human and canine!

As he gets older he steadies down and is biddable and happy to please you; he will always greet you as a long-lost friend, even if you've only been gone five minutes! His main interest in life is always to be out in the country hunting, or galloping for sheer joy. A bitch has all these characteristics with one exception – although she loves her canine friends, she is often timid with strange dogs and will come to her owner's heels if one is pestering her, for protection. The other most important thing in a Setter's life is to be near his master or mistress wherever they are.

Movement. Good movement goes with good conformation; if a dog is well-made, it ought to move correctly. A Setter should stride out straight and true – 'daisy cutting' in front, with no tendency to hackney action; the powerful hindquarters should drive the dog along in straight forward thrusts, with no crossing legs or pushing feet out sideways. The Irish Setter should be a stylish mover, with a proud head carriage, and happily waving tail.

The breed standard of the Irish Setter Club of America is officially approved by the American Kennel Club. It is somewhat different from the English standard, in both descriptions and details, and also some breed points. For example, there is a paragraph on 'Size' which includes the 'ideal' height and weight. There are also paragraphs on 'Gait' and 'Balance' which are not in the original English standard of the breed.

The breed standard of the American Kennel Club is reproduced here with their kind permission.

Irish Setter Breed Standard of America

General appearance. The Irish Setter is an active, aristocratic bird-dog, rich red in color, substantial yet elegant in build. Standing over two feet tall at the shoulder, the dog has a straight fine, glossy coat, longer on ears, chest, tail and back of legs. Afield he is a swift-moving hunter; at home, a sweet-natured, trainable companion. His is a rollicking personality.

Head. Long and lean, its length at least double the width between the ears, the brow is raised, showing a distinct stop midway between the tip of nose and the well-defined occiput (rear point of skull). Thus the nearly level line from occiput to brow is set a little above and parallel to, the straight and equal line from eye to nose. The skull is oval when viewed from above or front; very slightly domed when viewed in profile. Beauty of head is emphasized by delicate chiseling along the muzzle, around and below the eyes, and along the cheeks. Muzzle moderately deep, nostrils wide, jaws of nearly equal length. Upper lips fairly square but not pendulous, the underline of the jaws being almost parallel with the top line of the muzzle. The teeth meet in a scissors bite in which the upper incisors fit closely over the lower, or they may meet evenly.

Nose. Black or chocolate.

Eyes. Somewhat almond-shaped, of medium size, placed rather well apart; neither deep set nor bulging. Color, dark to medium brown. Expression soft yet alert.

Ears. Set well back and low, not above level of eye. Leather thin, hanging in a neat fold close to the head, and nearly long enough to reach the nose.

Neck. Moderately long, strong but not thick, and slightly arched; free from throatiness, and fitting smoothly into the shoulders.

Body. Sufficiently long to permit a straight and free stride. Shoulder blades long, wide, sloping well back, fairly close together at the top, and joined in front to long upper arms angled to bring the elbows slightly rearward along the brisket. Chest deep, reaching approximately to the elbows; rather narrow in front. Ribs well sprung. Loins of moderate length, muscular and slightly arched. Top line of body from withers to tail slopes slightly downward without sharp drop at the croup. Hindquarters should be wide and powerful with broad, well-developed thighs.

Legs and feet. All legs sturdy, with plenty of bone, and strong, nearly straight pastern. Feet rather small, very firm, toes arched and close. Forelegs straight and sinewy, the elbows moving freely. Hind legs long and muscular from hip to hock, short and nearly perpendicular from hock to ground; well angulated at stifle and hock joints, which, like the elbows, incline neither in nor out.

Tail. Strong at root, tapering to a fine point, about long enough to reach the hock. Carriage straight or curving slightly upward, nearly level with the back.

Coat. Short and fine on head, forelegs and tips of ears; on all other parts, of moderate length and flat. Feathering long and silky on ears; on back of forelegs and thighs long and fine, with a pleasing fringe of hair on belly and brisket extending onto the chest. Feet well feathered between the toes. Fringe on tail moderately long and tapering. All coat and feathering as straight and free as possible from curl or wave.

Color. Mahogany or rich chestnut red, with no trace of black. A small amount of white on chest, throat, or toes, or a narrow centered streak on skull, is not to be penalized.

Size. There is no disqualification as to size. The make and fit of all parts and their over-all balance in the animal are rated more important. Twenty-seven inches at the withers with a show weight of about 70 pounds is considered ideal for a dog; the bitch 25 inches, 60 pounds. Variance beyond an inch up or down to be discouraged.

Gait. At the trot the gait is big, very lively, graceful and efficient. The head is held high. The hindquarters drive smoothly and with great power. The forelegs reach well ahead as if to pull in the ground, without giving the appearance of a hackney gait. The dog runs as he stands; straight. Seen from the front or rear, the forelegs, as well as the hind legs below the hock joint, move perpendicularly to the ground with some tendency towards a single track as speed increases. But a crossing or weaving of the legs, front or back, is objectionable.

Balance. At his best the lines of the Irish Setter so satisfy in over-all balance that artists have termed him the most beautiful of all dogs. The correct specimen always exhibits balance whether standing or in motion. Each part of the dog flows and fits smoothly into its neighboring parts without calling attention to itself.

7
Setters at Work

by Auriel Mason

The working Setter without any doubt is a very old breed being mentioned in books as long ago as the fifteenth and sixteenth centuries as a dog being used to find game birds. We can take it as fact that the Setter and Spaniel were very interwoven in those days, and gradually certain lines or strains were developed to suit the owner and his estates, and indeed even during the eighteenth and nineteenth centuries large landowners both in Ireland and Great Britain would often keep their own strain and would rarely introduce outside blood lines. In the twentieth century the Irish Red Setter should conform to the breed standard but the dog which has been bred basically from working stock tends to be smaller than the Irish Setter which has for many generations been bred solely to exhibit on the show bench, but providing each is sound and properly proportioned a slight variation in size is of no consequence. However, whatever the Irish is bred for, be it as a companion, show-dog or working gundog, we must never lose sight of its original physical and mental requirements which, if we wish to preserve the true Irish Setter, are just as important today. All the grace and charm of this breed has been written about in previous chapters but no one can fully appreciate their beauty until they have witnessed them doing the job for which they were originally evolved, which is hunting, finding and pointing wild game birds in open places, such as moorland and stubble fields.

It is important to remember to breed for the correct conformation of the Irish Setter, since only a dog which is properly put together can stand up to the type of work which it is required to do. A dog with a good shoulder will be able to go on galloping long after a poor-shouldered dog will have given up. Equally a dog needs well-sprung ribs, giving plenty of heart and lung room, four well-set-on legs to give the dog the correct balance for when it is negotiating difficult ground. All this makes the difference between a dog which appears to flow over its ground tirelessly irrespective of uneven going whether it be unbaled lines of straw, deep heather with hidden stones, or steep hillsides with gullies. In contrast the dog with cow hocks, narrow between the front legs, slab sided with ungainly long legs and no depth of chest would tire rapidly and would be incapable of hunting effectively. The dog intended to work should not only have the right conformation but all the necessary attributes which make it capable of being trained. Indeed a group of men in Ireland after the Second World War when sport could be thought of seriously again, had the foresight to seek out dogs with those special qualities and breed them together so assuring the working Irish Setter's future.

No matter how good in conformation and physical fitness a dog may be it will be completely useless for training for work if it lacks a good brain which in turn enables it to use its 'nose', and intelligence to co-operate with its handler. Gervase Markham writing in 1655 describes their work as follows:

> A setting dogge is a certaine lusty land spannell taught by nature to hunt the partridges before and more than any other chase whatsoever, and that with all eagerness and fierceness, running the fields ever so lustily and busily as if there was no limit on his desire and furie; yet so qualified and tempered with art and obedience, that when he is in the greatest and eagerest persuite, and seems to be most wild and frantike, that even thus one hem or sound of his master's voyce makes him presently stand, gaze about him, and looke into his master's face, taking all directions from it, whether to procede, stand still, or settle. Nay, even when he has come to the very place where his prey is, and hath, as it were, his nose over it, so that it seems he may take it up at his own pleasure, yet is his temperance and obedience so made and framed by arte that presently, even on a sudden, he either stands still or falles down upon his bellie, without daring once to open his mouth, or make any noise or motion at all, till that his master come unto him and thus proceedes in all things according to his directions and commandments.

How beautifully this describes the work performed by the bird dog.

It is believed that the 'setting' dog was bred in the time before guns were used. Apparently the dog hunted and pointed its birds as today, and as now would take its handler in to its quarry and crouch or 'set' or sit while a net was flung over the birds – hence the name 'Setter'.

The work of an Irish Setter is the same as that of an English Pointer, and the English or Gordon Setters whether it be for field trials or shooting or both. In essence they all hunt methodically and systematically to locate birds by scent, then point or 'set' them and ultimately 'flush' them, i.e. put the birds to flight, all in such a manner that they can be shot. To achieve this the handler with the 'guns' following on either side, walks in the middle of the land known as the 'beat' being worked by the dog. With the wind usually blowing into the handler's face, the dog is sent away at right angles to the handler and gallops across the wind questing as he travels. At a distance decided upon by the handler the dog turns and comes back towards the middle of the beat and then progresses along the same line but now on the opposite side of the handler and continues this pattern of left to right and right to left. The turning point may be a barrier such as a hedge, wall, fence or stream, or the dog may be turned with a whistle to indicate to him the width of his beat which he will keep to thereafter. During the turn the dog pulls forward some yards. This system of working is known as quartering.

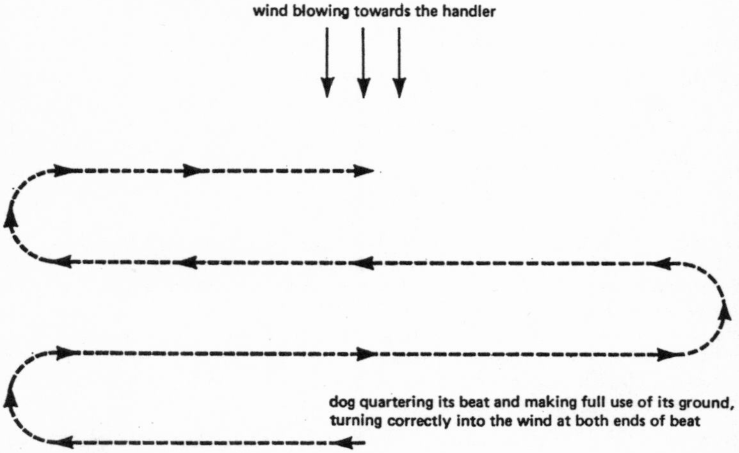

Fig. 13 Quartering. The beat may be anything from 200 to 400 yards or more wide depending upon the type of cover and the quantity of birds.

The scent of game birds is carried on the air by the wind so a Setter must carry its head well up to pick up this scent and should never drop its nose to the ground and follow foot scent. When the dog scents birds it should 'freeze' on 'point' and wait on that spot while the handler walks to it. The 'guns' are then positioned on either side of the dog, which is then given permission to walk forward with the handler at its side until it flushes the birds. Meanwhile the 'guns' will also be moving up keeping in line with the handler so as to be in a good position to shoot at the birds. When the birds fly the dog must drop as flat as possible, so as not to impede the 'guns' shooting at the birds and thereby ensure its own safety. After the 'guns' have reloaded the dog is asked to 'work out the point' until it is satisfied that all the birds have been put to flight. To 'work out a point' is for the dog to move cautiously from side to side over a very limited distance just wide enough to pick up the scent of any remaining birds. These may sit tight enough for the dog to point or get up quickly, in which case the dog must drop as before giving the guns freedom to shoot. This is repeated until there are no birds left, which will be indicated by the dog dropping its nose to the ground and wagging its tail rapidly. The dog should now be called to heel and put on a lead. The shot birds can then be picked up by a retrieving dog before the party moves forward to start hunting again with the Setter.

To achieve perfection a great deal of careful rearing and training has to take place. Confidence in man starts with the new-born puppy and must continue throughout its life so that a dog will give of its best for the handler. With consistent correct training the dog will know when it is doing the right thing and be prepared to gallop hard and fast concentrating fully on the search for game. The handler must have equal confidence and trust in the dog, so that both man and dog work as one unit, knowing that with the slightest pip on the whistle, raised hand or a mere whisper the dog will respond instantly and with pleasure.

The potential working dog must be grown correctly. It is no good growing him fast and soft as a hothouse plant. The handler must aim for the dog to acquire a fit well-balanced body with an alert quick-thinking brain. This will only be achieved with the right amount of exercise and food. Never over-tire or bore the youngster so that it lacks interest – make every outing a pleasure. Be consistent with every command and instruction right from the first time you take it out. Teach it to work its ground, to stop to your whistle, to sit and wait, to return to you, to watch you for hand signals. Praise it and admire it on all its successful achievements. All Irish Setters would benefit from such early training, even if they are never to smell game, or be used for working.

Do not introduce a puppy to wild game until you have got it going well and it is obeying your commands. It will need your help when it finds birds for the first few times, so that you can teach it how to behave after it 'points'. It could so easily rush in to the newly found scent or merely creep to it, but neither would be satisfactory as it might then flush the birds before the guns are in a position to shoot, or the handler there to insist on it dropping to rising birds. It is better to do the right thing from the start rather than do the wrong thing and have to be corrected. Interest in finding game birds will at this stage be uppermost in the dog's mind, so that teaching it to ignore rabbits, sheep and any other livestock should be fairly easy – but it must be done. Sitting hares may be ignored, but the pointing of sitting hares is permissable and they should then be handled in the same way as birds, but hare lining (that is dropping the nose and following foot scent) is a very bad trait and must be stopped, while hare chasing is unforgivable. In some parts of the country many hares are seen running about, and these can be very distracting for a hunting dog which must completely ignore them, and continue to work its ground systematically. By the time a dog is a year old it should have a good idea of what it is expected to do but it will still be very inexperienced. Only time and work will produce the seasoned veteran, that is a dog you can trust, hunting, galloping hard, finding birds and pointing them unhesitatingly, and waiting 'on point' indefinitely. Such a dog never potters on old scent or false points, but gives pure pleasure to the handler.

In the initial training of the young dog it is advisable to have the wind blowing into the handler's face to give the dog every chance of catching any scent, also it will enable the dog to keep to a good pattern of ground work. Later it must learn to cope with side winds (cheek wind).

The following diagram indicates the pattern of quartering a dog uses when the wind is at an angle on the left of the direction the handler is walking.

Whenever possible the dog will, as shown in the diagrams, keep its nose into the wind. To do this when working down wind the dog tends to start by taking in a large piece of ground and

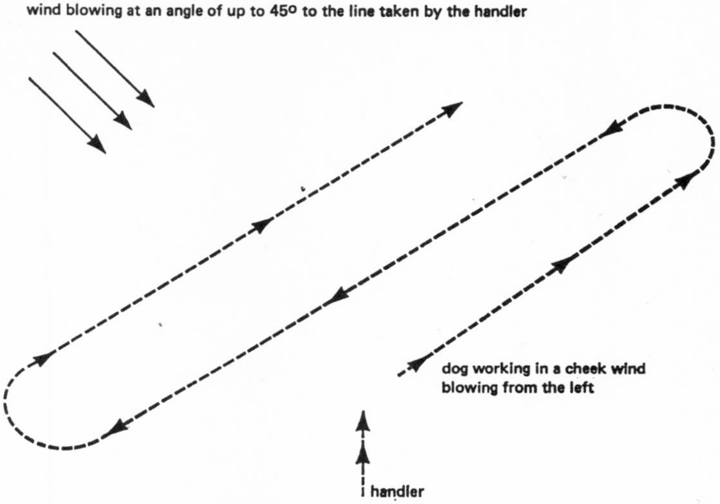

Fig. 14 Pattern of quartering. This is the method of working in a cheek wind, which can be blowing from one side or the other up to 45 degrees from the centre line of the beat.

then brings its quartering back towards the handler, thereby keeping its nose into the wind. However, there is more risk of birds being 'flushed' when working such a pattern.

The wind certainly plays a very important role in the life of bird dogs. It can be as variable in strength and direction as it is possible to imagine, even during one day's working, thus making scenting conditions just as variable. Sometimes a dog will be faced with a cold biting dry north-easterly wind hardly carrying any scent at all, especially if the ground has very short herbage, while another time a blustery wind at one moment brings scent in from a quarter of a mile away and yet the next moment when the wind has dropped the scent has gone. Conditions are also difficult with a wind which swings in all directions or a hot dry wind with no scent or when there is no wind at all and so no scent. Further problems arise with the wind which scurries round hills or broken ground leaving pockets with no wind and no scent, or with the wind which blows the scent above the heads of the dogs when working up the face of a steep hill. Deep gullies, large holes, woodlands or tall hedges all deflect the wind and cause a dog to

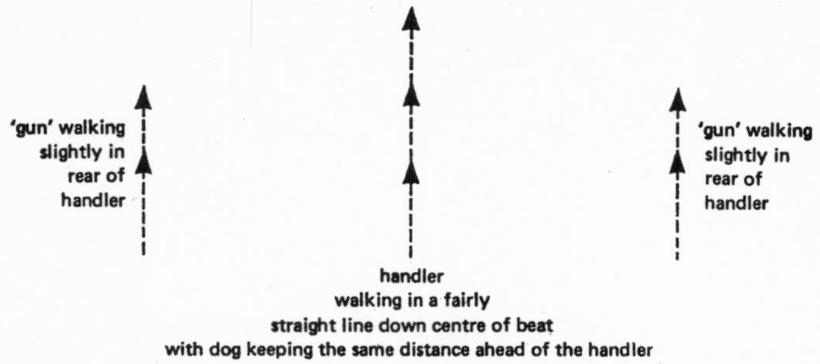

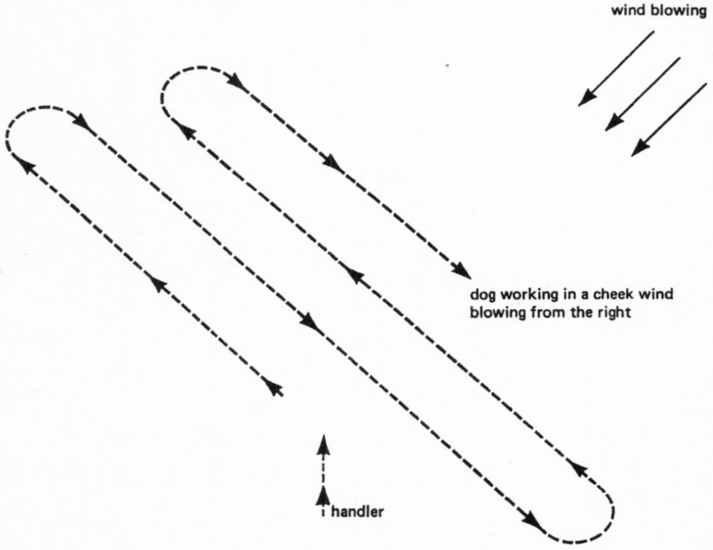

Fig. 15 If the wind is blowing from the right-hand side, the pattern would be slanted the other way, as shown here.

turn differently when nearing them. Examination by dangling a handkerchief to catch the wind or observing the smoke from a cigarette will show the difference in wind direction near such obstacles. Various ground covers and humidity do alter the intensity of smell from game birds, while it is scant from a dry stubble field it is much better in a lush green grass field.

With such variable conditions for a dog to work under, it is only to be expected that sometimes it will be able to 'point' birds a hundred yards away and yet half an hour later or in the next

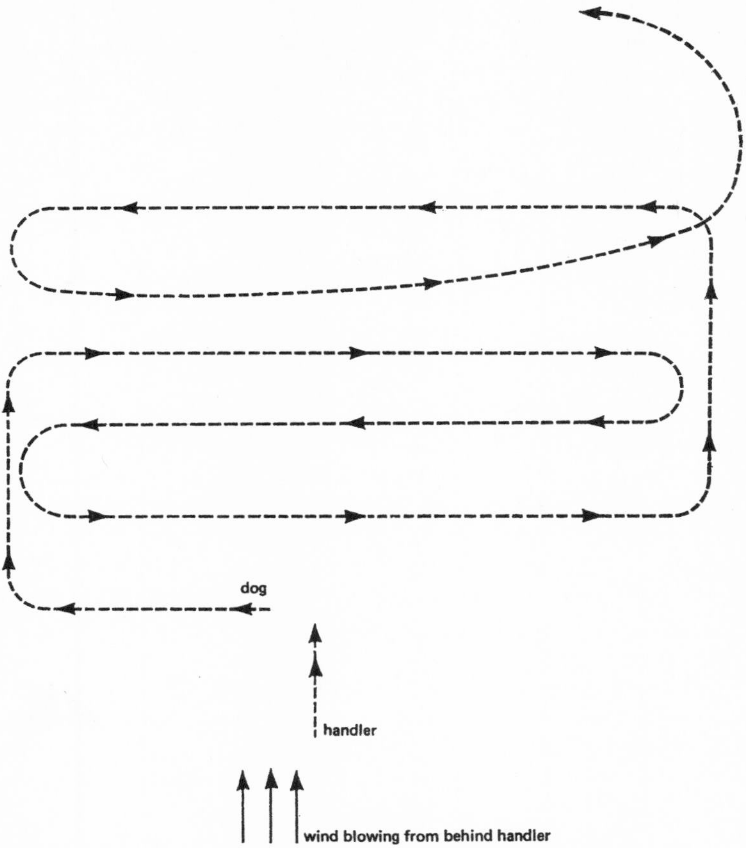

Fig. 16 There are also occasions when the wind is coming from behind the handler – a down wind – when the working pattern would be as above.

field it may be on top of its game before getting a whiff of scent. If your dog runs into game or misses birds, do analyse the conditions before condemning it.

While the training of a dog for field trials or shooting is basically the same the different conditions at a trial from those experienced when out shooting cause different reactions both in dog and handler. At a field trial two dogs run at the same time, they may never have met before or may be of different breeds. Trials may bring out the best competitive spirit in some dogs which then try to take the 'forward cast' when working their ground, while others may be adversely affected by the excitement of seeing so many dogs and handlers or may be distracted by the other handler's whistle. On shooting days there is no nervous tension or jealousy, as usually only one dog is working at a time, and the handler can be more relaxed as he has only his own dog to watch.

Field trials, all run under Kennel Club rules, are held in the spring, summer and autumn. They are organized by a number of separate clubs, and the dates and locations are announced in the *Kennel Gazette*. The Irish Setter Association of England in conjunction with the Setter and Pointer Club has for many years held a field trial on grouse at Shap during July, where there is, amongst other stakes (i.e. competitions) an Open Stake confined to Irish and Gordon Setters. The International Gundog League also run separate breed Open Stakes as well as those open to all breeds of bird dogs. The spring trials (April) are held on partridge and pheasant in the south and east of England, the summer trials on grouse (July) are in the north of England and Scotland (August) and the autumn trials on partridge and pheasant (September) are again in the south and east of England.

The awards from all the trials are recorded in the Stud Book. The Clubs are privileged to use land lent to them by landowners who generously allow the trials to take place on their shoots, and their interests must always be respected by both competitors and spectators. Land for trials must have sufficient game and plenty of cover. In the spring the cover may be young cereal crops and grass leys, while in autumn it is often long or unbaled straw left after harvest. Root crops are not suitable as too much noise is created when moving through them by both dog and followers, also the birds tend to run between the rows. The grouse trials are held on heather moors shortly before the start of the grouse shooting season (12 August) and sometimes problems are experienced following late spring hatchings, when the young birds (cheepers) are not strong enough to fly by the time the trials commence. It is necessary for trials to be completed not later than 5 p.m. to ensure that broods that have been disturbed during the day can collect together for safety and settle and feed before night-fall. All particulars of field trials, stakes to be run, together with conditions of entry can be obtained from Club Field Trial

Secretaries. Each trial always provides an Open or All Aged Stake for Pointers and Setters, and usually a Novice or Non-winner Stake, also there are Stakes for puppies born in the previous calendar year. There are Open Stakes for single breeds, and occasionally Brace Stakes, when one handler works two dogs of the same breed and in one ownership as a brace. The winning of two Open or All Aged Stakes, one of which must be for both Setters and Pointers, gives a dog the title of Field Trial Champion. However, there is the Champion Stake held alternately in England and Scotland with entry conditions laid down by the Kennel Club and the winner of this Stake gains its title. Any field trial meeting may be cancelled before or on the day if weather conditions are unfavourable. Usually heavy rains or high winds are the cause of cancellations since it would be harmful to disturb birds under such conditions. Sometimes low cloud and lack of visibility cause a trial to be abandoned, even in the middle of a Stake. 1976 made a variation on reasons for cancellation as owing to the prolonged drought the grouse had left the moor.

Irrespective of the number of Stakes being held during the day the total number of dogs will be restricted to about twenty brace to allow the judges sufficient time to see enough of the running of each dog. All participants meet at the appointed place and time to receive programmes showing in what order each brace of dogs has been drawn to run. The estate gamekeeper followed by judges, secretaries, stewards, gun, handlers, dogs and followers then move off to the particular field or moor chosen to start the day's proceedings.

The first brace of dogs are called for and the handlers told by the judges the beat to be worked. Distinctive coloured collars may be used to distinguish between dogs which are very similar in colour or appearance. The judges try to run each brace of dogs with a similar wind direction, and where possible each brace is run for between ten and fifteen minutes unless either or both make a bad mistake. When the dogs are set away they should make a pattern as shown here with the dog on the left making its first cast to the left and the dog on the right making its first cast to the right. The pattern, however, is not always as regular as shown. Sometimes a dog will work a wider 'beat' than the other or may be much faster, again one dog may stay pottering on old scent, or one dog may follow the other. As will be seen from this sketch the handlers

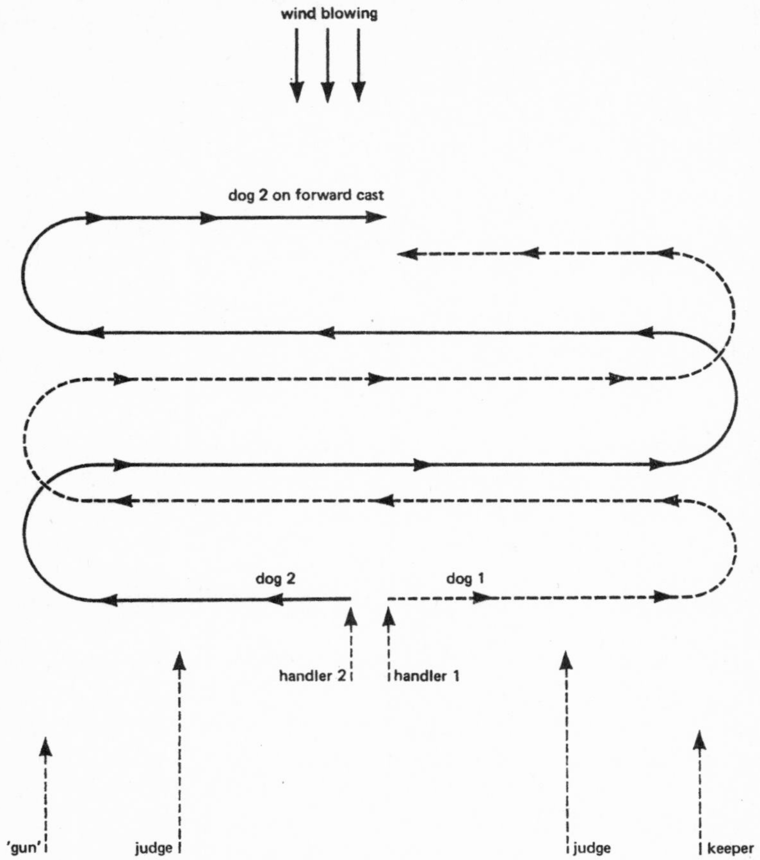

Fig. 17 Pattern for brace of dogs.

walk fairly close together in the middle of the 'beat' and often the judges are on either side of them. When the dogs are running their leads must not be carried in the hand and followers must keep noise and talking to a minimum to avoid distraction to the competing dogs or disturbance of the birds.

During the running of each brace of dogs the two judges watch every move the dogs make and all will be duly noted. Credit will be given to the dog which goes with a fine gallop and general good style, uses the full width of the beat, turns correctly at the ends of the beat, and when possible gets the 'forward cast' enabling it to wind birds before its running partner, points positively with a competent air, handles the birds correctly, works the 'points' out quietly and systematically, drops to birds and shot, 'backs' or 'honours' the other dog when it is pointing, i.e. stands on 'point' behind it, ignores rabbits, sheep and any other distraction, behaves correctly in all situations with hares, is easy to control during the whole run, and is a pleasure to watch. On the debit side the dog will be marked down if it runs without enthusiasm and drive, lacks polish and initiative, uses only part of the beat, or goes off the beat, bores straight into the wind, potters about on vague or old scent, drops its nose, false 'points', is unsteady on 'point' or is sticky on 'point', i.e. fails to move forward to flush the birds when instructed, chases hares or follows their foot scent, chases sheep or rabbits, flushes unpointed birds, chases or kills birds, rushes in front of the other dog on 'point', pinches 'points' instead of 'backing', behaves jealously or follows the other dog, interferes with the other dog's running, barks or bays when running, or is out of control and causes the handler to shout or whistle excessively. If a dog is out of control or has major faults the judges will ask the handler to collect his dog even if it has only been running for a few minutes. Under some circumstances there will be 'down wind' flushes which are not necessarily counted as faults, but a 'down wind' find is a very creditable achievement.

When a dog comes on 'point' the handler should hold up his arm to indicate to the judge that he is claiming a 'point'. The handler then walks up to his dog and waits for permission from the judge to allow the dog to walk forward and flush the birds. The gun will have moved up and will fire a blank shot as the birds rise, testing the dog for gun shyness or running in 'to shot'. The dog may be asked to work out the 'point' before being put on the lead. No attempt is made to shoot birds except at the Champion Stake. In this country Pointers and Setters are not asked to retrieve at field trials although they are on the Continent. After all the dogs have been run once, the judges will pick out all those showing particular merit and these will be drawn to run in a second round. Following the second round there may be a third round before the judges make their final placings for the awards. There are days when for various reasons, such as scent being so very poor, lack of birds or the best dogs running into trouble or such mediocre work throughout that the judges decide that no awards can be made. Aspiring handlers can learn much from studying the performance of dogs and the way they are handled at the trials but they are rarely in the right position to see as much as the judges and may not always be able to interpret exactly what has happened in a particular situation.

Every field trial day is different due to weather conditions, the lie of the land, the number and location of birds, with no two incidents ever quite the same. Each trial has something of fresh interest for those who appreciate the finer points of dog work even after years of following trials. The best days are often when there has been slight rain during the night and this has been cleared away by a westerly breeze with a touch of dampness in it, on such a day as this the work will be supreme. A dog pointing a whole covey of birds may appear most dramatic to the spectators but more credit should be given to the dog which is able to find a single bird. An incident remembered was when a young dog came firmly on 'point' and held its 'point' even while the other dog ran about in front of the dog on 'point' and could have been expected to have flushed any game that was there. After that dog was finally collected the young dog who was still firmly on 'point' was asked to produce its game, it moved forward one yard and put up a single cock grouse to the amazement of judges and spectators alike.

Dogs which have won at least one Challenge Certificate may be entered and given the opportunity to 'qualify' at a field trial. To 'qualify' a dog must show that it can work its ground with reasonable pace and style, be capable of acknowledging the scent of game birds, and must not chase flushed birds or be 'gun-shy' and of course must be under control. 'Qualifiers' are tested by themselves, but may also be entered in a Stake and approved if they put up a creditable performance. A dog may only be entered as a 'qualifier' on three occasions, and thereafter it can only qualify for its title by gaining at least a Certificate of Merit in a Stake. A dog which 'qualifies' and has three Challenge Certificates is given the title of Champion as opposed to Show Champion. These terms must not be confused with the title of Field Trial Champion. If a dog should gain both titles of Field Trial Champion and Show Champion it would be known as a Dual Champion.

Trained dogs may be used to locate game birds when falconing. This ancient sport is increasing in popularity.

In contrast to a field trial where a dog may have at the most two or three comparatively short runs, when shooting, the work throughout the day will be shared by only a few dogs. For a full day's work it is advisable to have about four dogs and use these in rotation, both dogs and handler must be very fit as the days may be long and arduous and on a grouse moor the hills may be steep and the heather may be deep, while the weather can be unbearably hot or soaking wet. Dogs will usually be run one at a time, but even so with a six- or seven-hour shooting day each dog will cover a tremendous number of miles. When they are working day after day for several weeks on a grouse moor great care is needed to keep them sufficiently well fed and in good condition. Dogs in their first shooting season must be handled with care on shooting days since too much work can tire them and spoil the pleasure they get from working while finding too many birds can over-excite them. It is advisable not to have more than one 'gun' shooting over a dog on its first outing, especially if it has only ever heard one shot at a time and perhaps has never seen game fall in front of it.

No matter how tiring, the results can be rewarding and memorable as for instance when at the end of a long, rather barren day we were making for the Land Rover and decided to run a dog. Although the heather was very poor giving no cover, the terrain flat and no noticeable wind, the dog came on 'point'. We were all amazed as we should have been able to see even a skylark on such land. Believing in the maxim 'always trust your dog' – it was given permission to go forward and we walked in line with the dog, firmly convinced by its rigid bearing that it must have grouse scent in its nose. We continued to walk on and on, it seemed endless, three guns all with their safety catches off, then finally the dog stopped and lowered its head. We had arrived at a patch of broken ground and a small gully with a little bit of heather overhanging it. Sure enough the dog was right, out popped one single grouse!

If you should have a piece of rough cover or land holding an odd pheasant, a few partridges, maybe a hare, a couple of wild duck, sometimes a snipe or two, what better than one man, his gun, and his Setter, to be taken out for an hour or two on a Saturday afternoon to work methodically with no fuss or bother, 'point' and take you in quietly to the game, behaving correctly whilst you shoot over it and even retrieve for you. Such pleasure can be yours if you have trained your Setter correctly to 'work'.

8

The Irish Setter Overseas

The beauty and character of the Irish Setter have become so universally appreciated that nowadays a contingent of the breed can be found at any important show in any part of the world.

America, where 'doing the circuit' involves weeks of time and thousands of miles, has the most registrations and their show calendar contains many comprehensively classified specialty events including the popular Irish Setter Club of America championship on the eve of the famous Westminster show. Classes start with three-month-old 'babes' and progress through a classification which enables enthusiasts to parade the promising and the proven – and then spend the next day at Westminster watching the (mainly) professional handlers exhibit the champions and other top quality adults eligible in the show's restricted classification.

Championship shows in Britain differ in a number of details from elsewhere. The mid-seventies saw a number of British shows stop giving prize money for economic reasons. In many cases, overseas shows have never done so, having given medals and ornaments and household goods. Judges in Europe have to assess each exhibit, write a 'crit' on all and award them excellent, very good, good or moderate. Irish Setter entries are booming to such an extent that four judges are needed for some club shows.

In some countries 'cages' are provided instead of show benches – roomy, clean and easily manageable, they are more practical for dog and exhibitor. Britain may have pioneered dog shows but, in a number of ways (as the following contributed material may show) the pupil may have overtaken teacher.

Dog shows on the Continent are run under FCI rules (Fédération Cynologique Internationale). At their international shows they award an international certificate as well as the national challenge certificate of the host country. Therefore, a dog winning the open or champion classes is eligible to compete for both

h. Ch. Wynjill Red Robin (*Michael* *akley*)

Sh. Ch. Cornevon Westerhuy's Dream. Stud dog of the Year 1979 (*Michael Oakley*)

. Ch. Marrona Meriel, Bitch CC and B.O.B. Cruft's 1974 (*Diane Pearce*)

A unique achievement. The first three places in a Open Irish and Gordon Setter Stake were won by three Acornbank Setters from the same litter; shown with their owner-breeder, Mrs. Auriel Mason

Sh. Ch. Timadon Ballywestow Festoon, with puppy later to become Sh. Ch. Timadon Kendel (*Deva Press*)

Aust. Ch. Quailmoor Royal
Leason (*Michael M. Trafford*)

Dutch Ch. Cornevon
Quiet Gentleman (*Piet Jacobs*)

Am. Ch. Starheir Aaron Ardee. The U.S.A.'s top winner in the history of the breed

N.Z. Ch. Farrahway of Redstone, best Irish Setter bitch N.Z. 1979. Multiple Best-in-Show winner championship shows

awards; however, a dog winning the youth class is ineligible to compete for the international certificate.

This is rather different in the USA where there is a 'special' class for champions only, where the dog winning this class can compete for best of breed only. Winners of the previous classes up to and including the open class, compete for the top award in each sex, gaining points towards their championship. They are called 'winners' dog and 'winners' bitch, who then compete for 'best of winners' and in turn with the 'specials' winner for best of breed.

Australia

The judging of dogs in Australia differs very little, if at all, from the method of English judging. There are, however, differences in the qualifications of judges, the organization of shows and the requirement for championship status.

Although most of the population of Australia live in and around the major cities, there are millions of people who do not do so. Due to the size of Australia it is quite impractical to expect country people to travel to these cities each time they wish to show a dog. This has given rise to the country shows where some 200 to 600 dogs may compete. Further, the various ruling bodies (and there is one for each State and Territory in Australia – eight in all) believe the good dogs in the country should be able to achieve championship status as well as the city dogs. Hence, country shows may recieve championship status even though only a very small number of dogs may attend (a championship show, once designated, offers challenge certificates to all breeds irrespective of the anticipated number of competitors).

Obviously, under these conditions it would be silly to grant a championship title on the basis of three challenge certificates. Instead, challenge certificates carry a number of points with them – five for being awarded a challenge and another one for each dog competing for the challenge up to a maximum of an additional twenty points.

A challenge certificate therefore carries a minimum of six points and a maximum of twenty-five and to achieve its championship a dog must total one hundred points from at least four challenge certificates under four different judges.

The system does have its merits and so far no better system has been designed which is fair to country folk. It is, however, abused by cityites occasionally who, with their dogs, go to the country shows in the hope of finding little or no opposition and a kindly judge.

As you can imagine, it is not economically possible for shows of 200 to 600 dogs to afford to fly in breed specialists to judge from as much as even 1000 miles. To overcome this problem, it is necessary to have many all-breeds judges (qualified to award challenge certificates in all breeds) and even more group judges.

As in the natural course of things, there would be very few people with this type of knowledge, training schemes have been devised and any would-be judge must now prove himself in theory and practical examination before he is given a licence to judge.

Comparing the system with the English system, it is obvious that the English judge in his specialist breeds will have a much greater depth of knowledge. On the other hand, his Australian counterpart will have greater breadth of knowledge of dogs in general and this must be an asset. It seems that both systems have some merit and the one that is right for the environment in which the judge is will be the correct one.

Championship shows in Australia differ in a number of respects. Due to the difference in climate there are no indoor shows and very few benched shows. Most show-grounds are crowded with groups of people sitting under large beach umbrellas with their dogs around them. In the winter months they may have a portable barbecue as well.

The classes of dogs vary somewhat too. Shows are limited to seven classes per dog per sex. The usual are:

Baby Puppy	three to six months
Minor Puppy	six to nine months
Puppy	six to twelve months
Junior	six to eighteen months
Intermediate	eighteen to thirty-six months
Australian Bred	over six months
Open	over six months

Baby puppies do not compete for the challenge certificates.

There are other classes more akin to the English classes but they are rarely used.

Only two shows in Australia draw more than 4000 entries. The Royal Easter Show (Sydney) with entries limited by qualification and the Royal Melbourne Show (no qualification required).

Each state has its own 'Royal' show and these are equivalent in importance to our Cruft's.

Between 1950 and 1970 the Parr Leyn kennel of Misses O. and N. Hinds of NSW accounted for ten royal challenges and five RES challenges. Their homebred Ch. Parr Leyn Red Garnet won best Setter at the first Pal International held in NSW. Ch. Parr Leyn Peggy O'Neill won the reserve challenge at Sydney Royal at nine months and in August 1962, a litter from their triple Royal CC winner, Ch. Parr Leyn Shanis O'Shea and Tatlow Irish Sonata included Parr Leyn Perry O'Shea who gained his title in nine shows and was retired at an early age to stud. He died in 1970 leaving behind some of today's leading stock.

Another, more recent, top kennel in New South Wales is Mr and Mrs R. G. Hamilton's Quailmoor strain. Graham and Norma Hamilton founded their kennels on Ch. Parr Leyn Symphone (a grand-daughter of Ch. Wendover Beggar). Symphone won CCs at Melbourne and Brisbane Royals, twice at Sydney Royal and, nearing six, was best gundog at Sydney Royal under Gwen Broadley in 1972. Quailmoors in 1976 won both CCs at Sydney Royal with Ch. Quailmoor Royal Leason and Ch. Quailmoor Fantasia (best gundog bitch). Leason was best in show at the Setter Club Championship Show in May.

In Queensland Graham Hall put his Listowel kennel clearly on the map with his foundation bitch, Rosebrook Honey Amber. A litter to New Zealand import, Coleraine Beggar Boy produced four champions, the most outstanding being Ch. Listowel Ember O'Burn CD, while a litter by Wendover Outlaw also yielded four champions. Dogs from these two litters became the foundation stock of two main Queensland kennels, Kelsherry and Sillsett.

A foundation bitch with quality both as an exhibit and as a brood gave Keith McCarthy (Taraglen) a quick lift to success. His bitch, Ch. Mavang Amber Glow, bred by Barbara Watt, probably had her greatest win when L. C. James gave her the CC and best gundog bitch at Melbourne Royal. Mated to the NSW dog, Ch. Greglyn Red Radiance, she produced Ch. Taraglen Toccata, a consistent winner and best gundog at Melbourne Royal.

South Africa

The influence of a number of imported Irish Setter dogs, largely from England, has done much to establish and improve South African bred Irish Setters and make them increasingly popular to the South African public.

The majority of Setters in the Transvaal are either pure Wendover or their combination with South African bitches, principally involving Mr Faye's Wendover Bachelor Boy and Wendover Bugle Call. Wendover Duggin resides in Natal and again the influence is largely Wendover.

In the Cape for many years the South African bred Donegal strain predominated, the owner and breeder, Mrs Hill importing regularly from the Hartsbourne line in England. (Mrs Hill was instrumental in setting up the Cape Gundog Club and was chairlady for many years.) Sadly through her death, the Donegal line was not continued, the only bitch regularly featuring in present-day pedigrees being SA Ch. Rumadre's Ruby O'Reily of Donegal owned by Mrs U. Poulton. By breeding to SA Ch. Kerry Dancer of Andana (imported from England) she incorporated Mrs Anderson's line and produced litter sisters, SA Ch. Alanna of Rumadre (owned by breeder) and SA Ch. Satana of Rumadre (owned by Mrs B. Simpson). Alanna's mating to an American import, Jo'etta Falacy produced SA Ch. Vanory of Rumadre.

The Cornevon strain was introduced by Mr L. Tichener with Cornevon Madonna and the subsequent importing of Cornevon Dreamer of Oakdale, now a champion, by Mrs B. Simpson.

In the mid-seventies there came some influence from the American strain of USA Ch. Bayberry Red Dust of Sherewood through the introduction of three offspring from Rhodesia by the Zambian bred bitch, Brackkin Honey but on the whole English bred Irish Setters are the type preferred by breeders in the Cape.

To summarize, the Transvaal and Natal are largely Wendover ground with Mr Faye's Wendover strain in Johannesburg and Mr McQuicken and Mrs Dwyer with Wendover or Wendover offspring by SA bred bitches; in the Cape Mrs U. Poulton with SA bred bitches by English and American sires, Mr Tichener with Cornevon and offspring, Mrs Simpson with SA bred bitches by imported Irish and English sires, and Mrs Wright with Wendover offspring combined with Australian imports. These are South Africa's most consistent breeders of Irish Setters in recent years although there are many breeders and owners with offspring from these strains.

Many shows take place on permanent agricultural show grounds but benching, though available, is seldom used by exhibitors, the norm being to erect your sun umbrella and fix the dogs near your deck chairs within view of the ring. Championship shows may be one- or two-day affairs depending on the number of judges and exhibits. Local shows are either an afternoon for a specialist club or a full day. Usually champions are not accepted for local shows. With few exceptions all shows are held outdoors. The number of Irish Setter entries varies considerably throughout the country, depending on the time of year and distances involved. There may be as few as five or six or as many as twenty in the open class when CCs are awarded.

There is usually a trophy donated for the best Irish Setter or best Setter at all-bred championship shows and often the CC winners receive a prize, such as bottles of wine, leads, glasses, donated by a sponsor or by the club concerned. Specialist clubs, such as the Cape Gundog Club, offer trophies for best Irish Setter pup, best Setter, best Irish Setter, and best opposite sex.

The important shows for the gundog group are the two specialist gundog shows, held by the Cape Gundog Club and the Gundog Club of Transvaal, and the Natal Gundog Club Championship Shows. Overseas gundog judges are usually appointed for these events. The other big show of the year is Goldfields Kennel Club Championship Show, South Africa's 'Cruft's'. Most shows are sponsored in part or in full by dogfood companies and various other interested companies or individuals.

The Transvaal and Cape gundog clubs both produce a regular periodical and field trials have been initiated in the Cape. Branches of the Natal and Transvaal clubs regularly hold fieldwork days and all three clubs hold show training classes.

Canada

One of the most successful Canadian kennels is McCamon Kennels in Saskatoon, Saskatchewan. Owner-breeder Sue Korpan used as her foundation stock the American Tirvelda bloodlines – typically tall, statuesque, very heavily coated, with a long, lean head and muzzle – which has brought many wins in the show-rings of Canada and the United States. Ch. McCamon's Royal Burgundy has had a number of outstanding wins.

In the same province is Mr Martin Kenney who, in his own words, began a programme in the mid-seventies of creating a new line by 'breeding the best of the English to the best of the American'. He imported Cornevon Swandance (Cornevon Timandra ex Margretwoods Caretaker) in 1974 and two years later mated her to Am. Ch. Starheir Aaron Ardee, producing top winners.

Of note in Alberta and British Columbia are Zodiac Kennels in Vancouver, BC, and O'Irish Kennels, formerly of Calgary, Alberta and now of Vancouver. Both used American foundation stock in their breeding programmes.

Many of the top winning dogs in Canada are from American bloodlines. Often potential breeders will purchase a top quality bitch south of the border and subsequently mate her back to an American dog.

The Canadian show scene closely approximates the American scene except that there are fewer professional handlers and it is not as crucial to have a professional handler in the best in show or group ring.

The growth of popularity in Irish Setters has, as in other parts of the world, produced problems of indiscriminate breeding. In Winnipeg newspapers regularly carry ten to twelve advertisements for Irish litters. Pups may be priced as low as 35 dollars and, in desperation, have even been given away. As a result reputable breeders, whose puppy sales have to recoup some of their costs, have had to think carefully before having even one litter a year.

New Zealand

Approximately 100 championship shows put on Irish Setter classes during the summer. They are held outdooors and benching is unknown except at the National Dog Show.

The National Dog Show, with its visiting internationally famous judges, is the main show of the New Zealand Kennel Club's show calendar. Held over three days in late August, it started in 1955 with an entry of 427 dogs, a far cry from its 1976 entry of 2850 with the Irish Setter contingent of eighty-four slightly down on the previous year.

The record of Irish Setters in best in show wins at the National Show is second only to German Shepherd Dogs (Alsatians), due mainly to Mrs R. Cummings. Her homebred Ch. Red River Blue Peter won in 1955 and she followed this with Ch. Red River Bouquet taking the supreme award again in 1965. The following year Mrs K. Butler's English import Ch. Wendover Gary of Acres went Best in Show.

The Irish Setter in New Zealand has steadily increased in popularity over the years and went from eighth to sixth place in 1975/76 with a rise from 511 registrations to 716.

The 'Redside' kennel, Mr H. Russell, now retired, gave the breed its first (and so far unequalled) winner of the New Zealand KC 'Dog of the Year' award, won in 1964 by Ch. Aggressor of Redside. His 'Redsides' have won many best in show awards and Ch. Cushla of Redside went best puppy in show at five and a half months after winning the baby puppy class.

A memorable hat-trick was produced by Mrs A. Millar's 'Erin' kennel. Her Ch. Sweet Sharleen of Erin won the bitch challenge at the National Show in 1973, 1974 and 1975.

Mr and Mrs F. Cantwell are well known in England and their 'Ballymoss' kennels are probably the largest in numbers in New Zealand Irish Setter circles. Primarily responsible for introducing the Wendover bloodlines into New Zealand, their imports have all made an impact on the breeding of Irish, particularly in the South Island. Their Ch. Wendover Sonata (Wendover Glade ex Wendover Lola) won the gundog group at the 1970 National Show and produced several very successful progeny, including Ch. Ballymoss O'Finnegin, who won the gundog group at the National Show in 1975.

Mrs R. Cummings' 'Red River' kennel has produced some of the most beautiful and successful Irish Setters in New Zealand. Although now retired from showing and breeding, 'Red River' still figures prominently in the pedigrees of the country's top Irish.

Brackenfield and Hartsbourne imports by Mrs O. Knight (Carnye) have proved very successful. Her big winners included Ch. Hartsbourne Hyacinth, Ch. Hartsbourne Sirius (by Comet) sire of many winners, and Ch. Moss of Brackenfield. The latter produced several Challenge winning progeny from her litter to Ch. Hartsbourne Telstar (Eng. imp.) owned by Mr and Mrs L. Frickleton. Telstar was the top winning Irish in 1975.

Two dogs which have had a strong influence on today's Irish Setter in New Zealand are Ch. Aggressor of Redside (Ch. Red River Son of Peter ex Ch. Arunside Acushla (Aust. imp.) and Ch. Wendover Gary of Acres. Gary, sire of the famous Sh. Ch. Wendover Gentleman before he left England, provided the basis for many successful New Zealand kennels and his influence through his sons and daughters remains very strong.

America

There are more Irish Setters in America than in any other country. In 1969 registrations were approaching 17000 and the Irish Setter ranked thirteenth in the country's registrations. Six years later, following an increased popularity perhaps due to Walt Disney's film *Big Red*, the breed had jumped into third place.

Showing begins early – there are often classes for baby pups, three months upwards – and the sheer size of the Irish Setter following is borne out by the numerous breed magazines (in colour) and the number of professional handlers. There are, however, breeders who prefer to 'go it alone' and show their own stock.

The history of the American Irish Setter is comprehensively described in William C. Thompson's *The New Irish Setter*. Suffice it to say here that one of their most famous imports was that of Elcho from Ireland in 1876. He was mated to over fifty bitches and had nine repeat matings to Palmerston's daughter, Rose.

Just under fifty years later another dog imported from Ireland (from J. A. Carbery) was to lead to one of the most famous 'nicks' in the breed's history. Paddy of Boyne and the American-bred Craigie Lea Mona produced four litters from which came six champions including Ch. Higgins' Red Pat (who won twenty-four best in shows, forty-three best in group and seventy-four best of breed awards) and Ch. Higgins Red Coat (who sired thirty champions).

Among Red Coat's influential sons were Ch. Milson O'Boy, Ch. Kinvarra Son of Red Coat and Ch. Redwood Russet of Harvale. Milson O'Boy was not only a great show-dog but he also founded many well-known kennels such as Rosecroft, Knightscroft and Caldene. Kinvarra Son of Red Coat helped establish the famous Kinvarra kennel which, begun by Lee Schoen in 1932, figures in so many American pedigrees. His Ch. Kinvarra Kermit had sired twenty-nine champions when the outbreak of war stopped his flourishing show and stud career.

Kermit's grandson, Ch. Tyrone Farm Malone II followed in his footsteps at Kinvarra after the war, and he sired twenty-five champions. Mr Schoen is a great believer in English bloodlines and has imported many Irish which figure in many of the pedigrees of Kinvarra and Tirvelda champions. Although he now breeds few litters, Mr Schoen maintains an active interest in the Setter scene on both sides of the Atlantic.

Mr Schoen was a guiding light in the starting of the Tirvelda Kennels when its owner, Ted Eldredge, at fourteen years old, asked him to bring back a bitch from England. Arriving at ten months, Mollie of Gadeland was to gain her title and prove a very prepotent brood. Mr Eldredge, whose Tirveldas are still at the top in the 1970s, considers he is still producing the same type as Mollie. His latter-day great stud dog Ch. Tirvelda Michaelson was producing semen for artificial insemination almost to the time he was put down at fifteen and seems set to surpass the American record of getting forty-one champions.

The Nilsen's Thenderin Kennel was founded on Ch. Kinvarra Portia, who produced five champions in one litter, and twelve altogether. She rates as one of the great broods of all time. Thenderin Kennels have bred over one hundred champions.

The Webline Kennel, owned by the Webbs, was made famous by Ch. Innisfail Color Scheme CD, both as a show-dog and a leading stud; he sired twenty-five champions.

Belgium

The standard was high and Irish were successful in both the field and the show when the Irish Setter Club of Belgium was founded in 1899. The most influential kennel ('Forest') was owned by Mr Bertrand. However, the First World War put an end to the success of the Irish Setter in Belgium until the late 1960s when some high quality stock was imported from England by Mr P. Jacobs.

His foundation bitch came from a Dutch kennel, Hanke van

Wolmerum, who became a Dutch champion and also bred some lovely stock from the English imports. Mr Jacobs ('Lowfield') imported Dutch Ch. Joanma's Don (sired by Wendover Game), the litter brother and sister Guildwich Gulliver (who died young) and Dutch Ch. Guildwich Gen (both by Sh. Ch. Scotswood Barabbas), Dutch Ch. Scotswood Hotspur (by Int. Ch. Wendover Royalist) and Cornevon True Love (by Sh. Ch. Cornevon Prince Charming and Sh. Ch. Cornevon Primrose). True Love had an accident when young and could not be shown.

The Lowfield kennel has been instrumental in re-establishing the Irish Setter in Belgium to a high standard as is shown by its record in other countries, particularly neighbouring Holland. His import, Cornevon Quiet Gentleman (by Sh. Ch. Twoacres Troilus ex Sh. Ch. Cornevon Cinderella) is a Dutch champion and is perhaps the most successful of his English purchases, both as a show-dog and a sire. He won best in show at the Dutch Club Championship Show three years running and was the leading sire in Holland and Belgium in 1974 and 1975.

Holland

The Irish Setter Club of Holland was founded in 1915 but Irish Setters were being shown long before that.

Many present-day bloodlines stem from two bitches imported from England in the 1930s: Champion Hartsbourne Lucy W'35 and Ch. Hartsbourne Josephine W'36. They were imported by Mr van Hesterman and Mr Verwey.

Hartsbourne Lucy was by Rheola Benedict ex Hartsbourne Jewel. She produced Ch. Fial O'Cuchulain, who won CAC at the Amsterdam Winners show in 1937 and 1940.

Fial's litter sister, Grania O'Cuchulain, was the ancestress of Mej v.d. Sijde's famous Goldwyn strain, from which a line of champions have descended, the latest being Ch. Goldwyn's Lucy.

The 'Chestnut Garden' kennel is also descended from Hartsbourne Lucy, via Lilian of Sutherland. This successful kennel has produced many champions.

Ch. Hartsbourne Josephine was by Hartsbourne Hector, who was a half-brother to Hartsbourne Lucy. The daughter of Josephine, Fionna Laline of Sutherland, was the foundation bitch of the O'Cuchulain Setters, owned by Mr Hesterman. Several champions came down from this bitch line, including the famous Ch. Shandon O'Cuchulain. Mr van Hesterman later mated Shandon's sister, Bessie O'Cuchulain, to Wendover Koko, to incorporate a PRA-clear bloodline into his stock.

Mr Hoegan Dykhof was the owner of the successful Polyandrie's kennel, which goes back to Hartsbourne Josephine via his foundation bitch, Maise O'Cuchulain, who produced three champions.

Mr Alofs was the owner of the Shamrock kennel and also a famous judge on the Continent.

Mr van Gemert founded his very well-known kennel 'van Wolmerum' in 1960 with a descendant of the Shamrock Beatera line, Heike. This kennel imported four dogs from England: Hoobram Gay Boy, Brackenfield Tartar, Dutch Ch. Wendover Eelkes and Dutch Ch. Wendover Doetse. These dogs, particularly the latter two, have contributed towards making this strain so successful. Mr and Mrs van Gemert were the top breeders in the Irish Setter Club six times during the 1960s, and have bred or owned many champions.

The family Verlaan-Duynkerke, who own the prefix 'van de Westerhuy' imported several dogs, of the Cornevon strain, from England from 1970 onwards. Cornevon Malisa, litter sister to the British champion, Cornevon Mercury, won many CACs on the Continent, and had just reared her first litter when she was killed by a car at the early age of three. Fenfield Faust, who was by Sh. Ch. Cornevon Prince Charming, has sired some quality showstock, as well as winning well himself.

Mr and Mrs P. Roks of the 'Hunters Home' affix are among the top breeders and exhibitors of Irish in Holland. They have imported English stock, two of the most successful being Ch. Cornevon Starlight and Ch. Cornevon West Whirligig, top Irish Setter in Holland in 1979.

Mr and Mrs C. Hermes have successfully campaigned two English imports to their Dutch titles; Ch. Cornevon Starbill (litter brother to English Sh. Ch. Cornevon Stargem) and the bitch, Ch. Cornevon Raindrop, who was also the top Irish Setter in Holland in 1975.

9
Ailments

Routine hygiene and regular inspection

Keeping your dog as healthy as possible means regular weekly check-ups on eyes, ears, teeth, skin and coat, feet, nails, and anal glands. Hygiene is also vital to good health.

As a Setter grows up, it gets into a routine and any break from this may point to the start of an ailment, some hitherto undiscovered injury or discomfort, so it is important to know your dog and his habits well: this could one day save his life.

I had a greedy, six-month-old puppy called Honey who would eat anything, including apples, pears and plums (windfalls from our trees) and twigs, stones etc. One day she vomited three plum stones together! However, the point of this story is still to come.

One morning, while out on our routine run on the common, she appeared a little down in the mouth, was sluggish and kept lying down, which wasn't like her. Back at home she refused her lunch, drank a lot of water and was obviously uncomfortable. She kept changing her position in her bed and getting up to stretch. Part of the time she lay on her stomach on the cold floor and was looking progressively more unwell, so I took her to the veterinary surgeon. He felt her tummy and immediately said that she had swallowed a large round stone. Trust Honey!

However, it was not yet critical and he gave her a penicillin injection to combat any infection and said there was still time for her to pass it naturally. Zero hour was set at next day. If it was still there he would have to operate. Fortunately she got rid of it and when I took her back to the surgery she was in fine health and spirits – a different, more normal Honey. No ill effects, either.

Hygiene. You should keep your Setter in hygienic conditions for his – and your – health's sake. Food and water should be given fresh and clean, not left around to go stale and have flies leave their burden of disease upon it. Any excreta should be removed daily from the garden and these infected parts, plus habitual 'piddling' places should be doused regularly with diluted disinfectant.

The dog bed should be checked every day and washed out once a week and clean bedding put down. If you get trouble with parasites, dust the bed with flea powder before putting the bedding down.

General health. As I have mentioned in an earlier chapter, the best time to check your dog's general health is when you are grooming him. The *eyes* should be bright and free from any thick discharge, although many setters have a slight transparent discharge, noticeable in the mornings, in the corner of the eyes. This should be gently wiped away with a piece of damp cotton wool. If the eyes are inflamed in any way, they should be examined and treated by a veterinary surgeon.

Ears should be clean, free from dirt, wax or inflammation. If not, ask your veterinary surgeon to recommend a suitable ear lotion or other treatment.

Check the *teeth and gums* for tartar or inflammation. If you find that chewing bones, hard biscuits, etc., doesn't keep your dog's teeth clean, you can clean them yourself with a soft toothbrush and warm water. There is even a special canine toothpaste available. However, if the teeth become heavily coated this inflames the gums and causes discomfort, loose teeth and even abscesses, and should be dealt with by the veterinary surgeon.

Skin and coat should be clean and healthy, with no scurf, red patches of irritation, or any sign of parasites. If a dog persistently scratches and nibbles then is the time to get out your fine toothcomb and go through the coat carefully. If fleas are the cause, you will probably find the 'flea dirt' first – small bits of black dirt – on the back and around the base of the tail. You may also find a flea but as dog fleas are a copper red colour they don't show up against an Irish coat! Lice and ticks are fairly easy to spot when you are combing against the lay of the coat to expose the skin. They do not charge around like fleas but stick their heads into the poor dog and suck blood. All these pests can be destroyed by a good flea powder, insecticidal spray or a bath with an insecticidal shampoo. If these don't work, your veterinary surgeon will supply a suitable coat dressing. In these circumstances, remember to vacuum the dog-bed, also everywhere the dog could have been, in order to account for any eggs laid in corners etc. These are very difficult to eradicate if you have wall-to-wall carpeting and so it is sensible to give your dog some anti-parasitic treatment about every two weeks until you are sure he is clear. Beds and blankets, etc., should always be washed and some flea powder dusted in the bottom of the bed.

To get back to causes of irritation, if your fine toothcomb has not come up with anything as obvious as the above, then a trip to the veterinary surgeon is indicated. He will diagnose the problem which could be many things such as an allergy to something, or mange, eczema, dandruff etc.

Always keep to the manufacturer's instructions when using insecticidals.

Feet should be inspected for small stones, or bits of biscuit stuck between their pads. In muddy weather, unless washed in warm water after a walk, bits of wet mud will dry into stone-hard balls between his toes.

Interdigital cysts are rather painful and can cause lameness. A cyst appears between the toes as a small red bump and becomes quite swollen and full of pus. The foot should be held in hot water and Epsom salts four or five times daily until the cyst bursts. Veterinary help should also be sought. These cysts are difficult to eradicate completely as some dogs are more susceptible to them than others.

Nails should be inspected every two weeks and, if too long, should have the 'hooks' cut off; be very careful not to cut the quick as this bleeds and hurts the dog so much that he probably won't let you anywhere near his feet again in a hurry!

Dew-claws on a Setter's front legs are easily missed, as the feathering hides them; if left to grow unimpeded, they will curl right round and enter the dog's leg, causing much pain. So check them along with the regular nails and cut the points off at the same time.

Anal glands sometimes need emptying. Your dog will show symptoms like dragging his bottom along the ground, licking his anus, leaping up as though stabbed; sometimes you will smell them if bad and it is an awful smell! Your veterinary surgeon will deal with these for you. If these glands become infected, your dog can end up with a nasty abscess or even an operation, so never neglect to treat them.

These 'dos' and 'don'ts' are well worth pursuing, as in the long run you could be saved a long drawn-out ailment or illness, with countless visits to the veterinary surgery and a large bill!

Puppy ailments

Roundworms. All puppies are born with roundworms and breeders should worm their litters at the earliest possible age that is safe for the pups, using a recommended vermifuge or one obtained from their veterinary surgeon. I worm my pups for the first time not later than three weeks old and again seven to ten days later, and so on until there is no trace of worms. I often worm a litter four times before eight weeks of age. When puppies go to their new homes, it is necessary for them to be wormed again when they've been there a couple of days, with another dose ten days after the first. If there's no sign of worms, they can be left for a month before their next dose. It is best for the puppy's owner to be advised by the veterinary surgeon as to what to use, size of dose and how often.

Tapeworm. The tapeworm does not often occur in puppies and is much more serious. Dogs cannot directly infect each other with tapeworms, as it requires an intermediary host, most commonly a flea, but also rabbits. When the dog eats a flea then the chances are that he now also has a tapeworm, which shows the importance of keeping him free from fleas! Apart from losing condition, the easiest way to detect the tapeworm in your dog is to check the anus and feathering around his tail and back legs for the tapeworm segments which are expelled along with the faeces and look like grains of rice. The tapeworm must always be treated by a veterinary surgeon as quickly as possible.

Virus diseases and inoculations. Inoculations should be given against Distemper (including Hardpad), Hepatitis and the two forms of Leptospirosis: Leptospiral Jaundice and Canicola fever. Puppies should have the necessary injections at the age recommended by the veterinary surgeon. Annual booster doses are also advised. Uninoculated puppies or adults which contract any of these diseases have a fairly low survival rate.

Parvovirus, a new disease, appeared in 1978. It attacks in two different ways: puppies under five weeks old are affected in their hearts and almost always die of heart attacks. Dogs over that age suffer from violent diarrhoea and vomiting, which can include blood, a very bad sign. They dehydrate in a matter of hours and even if treated by a vet immediately can still die very quickly. As this disease is almost the same as cat enteritis, the Feline Enteritis vaccine has been used with success on dogs, but now an inactivated canine vaccine has been licensed for dogs. It is very important to have your dog inoculated against this new disease.

Tummy upsets. Some Irish Setters are prone to these and seem to have delicate digestions. Of course, puppies often eat such unsuitable things – anything they can lay their teeth on! Such as plastic toys, pieces of rag, nylons, rubber, sticks and stones etc. etc. Most of these are very bad for them, of course, and although many objects go straight through the puppy and are passed out with no trouble, there is always the odd time when he becomes ill and should be taken straight to the surgery, otherwise, you are in danger of a very sick or even dead puppy. It is advisable to remove all unsuitable objects from the vicinity of a young puppy for obvious reasons! He should have his own play things – safe ones – and no others. Various other things cause minor tummy upsets; worms, unsuitable food, indigestion etc. They can also be the forerunners of more serious things such as virus disease or gastro-enteritis so, when in doubt, consult your veterinary surgeon.

Diarrhoea. This often accompanies tummy upsets. It can be caused by eating too much liver, or drinking a lot of milk or some such minor thing that does not agree with your dog. It is best to withhold all food and milk for twenty-four hours and just give water, plus some mild treatment prescribed by your veterinary surgeon. Diarrhoea can also be a symptom of a more serious disease and where there is not an obvious minor cause, the animal should be taken to the veterinary surgeon for diagnosis and treatment.

Teething. Puppies lose their baby teeth and begin cutting their new adult teeth at around three and a half to five months old. During this period their gums are often swollen but Setters don't seem to suffer a lot of discomfort. However, they do need plenty of hard biscuits, bones etc. to chew on.

Many of the following ailments are applicable to puppies and the same applies to puppy ailments and adults.

General ailments

Tonsillitis. Irish Setters are prone to this malady; a puppy or youngster can have an isolated attack or it can be the first of many. A Setter can have chronically infected tonsils by two years of age. In this sort of case, the best plan is to have them removed. Several of my Irish have had their tonsils out and it has done nothing but good; from being fussy eaters, rather on the thin side, they all became good 'doers' with lovely bodies.

Symptoms of infected tonsils are lack of interest in food; in a mild case this is the only way it affects an Irish. They still gallop madly about on walks and play happily at home! However, if any of my Setters won't eat its dinner and there's no obvious reason why not, I look down its throat and if I see red tonsils then we take a trip down to the veterinary surgery. Tonsillitis always needs antibiotic treatment, no matter how mild a case.

When a dog has a severe attack, it is listless and coughs a bit and quite often runs a temperature and is obviously ill. Tonsillitis can also be a symptom of a serious virus disease.

Kennel cough is a general name for one or more viruses affecting the tonsils, throat and surrounding area; the dog has a constant irritation in its throat and coughs a lot, especially when getting up from a rest and walking around or when excited and greeting someone. Funnily enough, when out for a gallop, they don't cough at all! Typical Irish Setter – half-dead, getting lots of sympathy at home, but if taken for a run, forgets all about being ill! Treatment for this condition consists of antibiotics to guard against any secondary infection; the virus runs its course and as long as there are no complications, the dog recovers and is perfectly OK. Old dogs and very young pups are more at risk than the middle age-group. Veterinary treatment is definitely necessary, and it is very important to keep your coughing dog away from others as the cough is highly infectious and can quickly be passed on in public places such as dog shows.

Indigestion is another type of tummy upset to which some Irish are susceptible, symptoms are noisy rumbling tummies, lack of interest in everyday routine (walks excepted), grass-eating. I allow the afflicted Setter to eat as much grass as is necessary and be sick etc. When this stage is finished, if a mild case, I give a large teaspoon of Milk of Magnesia; but if the dog is obviously under the weather, I give a dose of the tablets which my veterinary surgeon provides for this condition and within two to three hours the animal is fine. Your veterinary surgeon will provide a similar remedy.

Constipation. Doesn't occur often in Irish, unless they've been fed on too many bones or unsuitable food. A dessertspoon of Milk of Magnesia or some other mild laxative helps or a liberal helping of liver which nearly always softens or loosens a motion. If your Setter doesn't react to this treatment, a visit to the veterinary surgeon is necessary, as it may have a stoppage or some other trouble.

Stinging nettle feet. This occurs occasionally in puppies and young dogs whose feet and pads are still soft and tender, mainly in the spring when young nettles are easily walked upon. Symptoms are: the youngster is home from his walk and is lying down resting when suddenly he leaps up and rushes away, only to come back and try to dig up his bed frantically; when you examine his feet, the toes are extended with tension but apart from being pinker than usual, nothing much else to see. Some young Setters are driven nearly mad with it, and cry and thrash about trying to find some relief. I've tried putting various solutions and lotions on the feet, but most things just make it worse, so my veterinary surgeon gives me a small store of antihistamine tablets to keep by me and I give two to the dog at once. Then you have to just wait until they work and the dog relaxes. In bad cases, half an aspirin helps in addition to the antihistamines.

Sting. Bee stings don't usually improve much until you've located the sting and removed it. You probably wouldn't even know your dog was stung until the surrounding area becomes rather swollen – usually on the *lip* where the silly animal has been snapping at the bee, and now has a rather lopsided appearance in the face! Always examine the area carefully for the sting and pull it out when found. Antihistamines come in handy for all stings too, so give the Setter the necessary dose, and wait for it to work. The same goes for *wasp* stings, except that there is no sting to pull out. If the sting is in the mouth or throat, this can be dangerous and the dog should be taken to the veterinary surgeon immediately as the swelling can impede breathing.

Grass-seeds. Those such as wild barley or grass darts can be picked up on ears and travel right into the ear, where they can do untold damage if the dog isn't taken directly to the veterinary surgeon. Removal is always a case for the expert, as the unskilled can do more harm than good. There was once a lovely young dog of my breeding who had already won his Junior Warrant and a CC and had a glittering future. . . . He apparently got a grass seed in his ear but his owners didn't notice and by the time they did, the damage was done. The seed had penetrated his inner ear, his balance was affected and he carried his head permanently on one side. What a tragic waste. Grass-seeds can also enter dogs' feet between the toes. Incredibly, there have been cases of seeds getting into feet, travelling up the leg to the elbow – and then emerging! Mostly they start an inflammation which can turn into a nasty cyst or boil; this needs poulticing and veterinary treatment.

Snake bite. If your dog is unlucky enough to be bitten by an adder the most likely place is foot or leg. Apply a tourniquet to the limb (if it is a limb) and rush him to the veterinary surgeon. The tourniquet should be loosened every ten minutes. Prompt action is necessary.

Heatstroke. This is brought about by carelessness. Dogs should never be left in a situation where they cannot cool off. A house usually has a cool corner somewhere, preferably uncarpeted. A garden should have a patch of shade – if necessary, erect a man-made shade from a tarpaulin or similar. This also applies to kennels and runs. Fresh cold water should be constantly accessible. Cars, of course, are the chief offenders. Never leave dogs in a car, even with the windows down, in the heat of the sun. The car becomes an oven in a very short time. Every summer many dogs die from this lack of forethought which amounts to criminal negligence. Adequate arrangements for your dog's comfort and well-being should be paramount at all times. If your dog does get heatstroke get him into a cool place and apply cold water to the head, neck and shoulders. Give cold drinks and, if ice is available, apply an ice pack. In an emergency you can drop him into cold water up to his neck and pour cold water over his head.

Poisoning. Can cause shock, collapse and eventual death so immediate professional treatment is essential. If you know that the dog has only just recently swallowed the poison, you must make him sick, either by a piece of washing soda pushed down the throat, or by administering a strong salt solution. Common causes of poisoning are slug pellets and rat poison, such as Warfarin. If you have no idea when the poison was eaten and the dog is obviously ill, don't make him sick, just get him to the surgery quickly. A description of what the dog ate will obviously help the veterinary surgeon.

Wounds. Can be caused by dog bites, broken bottles, barbed wire, a bad fall, car accident etc. All but the small, clean cut, which will obviously knit together easily and quickly, must be tied up or covered over, and taken at once to the veterinary surgeon. If there is profuse bleeding or an artery cut, a tourniquet must be applied but should be loosened every ten minutes while waiting for veterinary treatment.

Vomiting. This is something that every dog does now and then when feeling a bit off colour. He will eat grass and then vomit bile and grass, feeling much better afterwards. If a dog vomits constantly, and is obviously ill, consult your vet quickly.

Accidents. If a dog is involved in a serious accident such as a road crash and is obviously badly injured and cannot move, get him out of the road and to the nearest veterinary surgeon for immediate attention. Surgery may be vital and essential time can be lost calling a veterinary surgeon to the scene. Be careful in tending the injured animal as he is liable to lash out in panic and bite anyone through pain and shock. Warmth is important so cover up the injured animal. If there is excessive bleeding, apply a tourniquet but loosen it every ten minutes until treatment commences.

Travel sickness. I have covered this in Chapter 3. The best remedy I know is Sealegs (for humans). One tablet (or two if bad) the night before the journey, or two or three hours before starting.

Eclampsia. Happens to a bitch nursing puppies usually around three weeks old when they are taking a lot of milk from her. She cannot replenish her low stock of calcium quickly enough and eclampsia manifests itself quite suddenly. Her eyes take on a glazed appearance and her movement becomes stiff-legged and goose-stepping, followed by staggering and finally collapse with continual twitching. Get her straight away to the veterinary surgeon for an intravenous injection of calcium; if this isn't done promptly, she can die. Eclampsia has been known to happen at other times, notably just before whelping. The treatment is the same.

Mastitis. Can happen when a nursing bitch has only a few puppies drawing off an abundant milk supply. Abscesses form on insufficiently-used teats making them extremely sore. Puppies have to be removed and hand reared, and mum needs immediate veterinary treatment. This doesn't happen very often, as nature usually reduces the milk supply to the necessary amount and if the owner is careful to feed correctly (i.e. relate the quantity of food and milk given to the demands on her) this problem should not arise.

Cystitis. Inflammation of the bladder in bitches which causes them to urinate frequently, and with much difficulty and pain. Traces of blood appear in the urine. It happens more often in older and spayed bitches and can usually be controlled by veterinary treatment.

False pregnancy. A frequent occurrence in Irish Setters but not often severe. After her first season, a young bitch will exhibit enlargement and even blue swelling around her teats. This will gradually disappear and near the nine weeks after her season, she may have a little milk in her glands. This will often right itself with no help from the owner. She will probably 'blow up' a bit in body and look quite fat, so when this happens reduce her food a little. Occasionally a bitch can have a severe attack and become psychologically disturbed, crying and making a bed; any small cuddly object she takes a fancy to becomes her baby and she has a lot of milk. In this case she needs veterinary treatment.

A bitch that has a mild false pregnancy can make an ideal foster mother (several of my bitches have done this). However, the severe case is a terrible nuisance and as such bitches make a habit of this after every season, even after having a litter, the only permanent cure is spaying.

Bed-sores. Not likely to happen with a properly cared-for dog but they can arise in bitches nursing pups. This is due to the change from the normal cushioned bedding arrangements to a whelping box. A Setter bitch nursing a large litter has to be in a large box, with often only newspaper or a thin flannelette sheet to rest on. All her weight when lying down falls on her elbows and the top of her hind legs and the hair may rub off and callouses develop. They can be rubbed with Vaseline or Lanolin ointment, but if they become open sores, veterinary treatment will be necessary. Usually only bitches with sensitive skins, who lack coat, have this trouble.

Metritis. Can develop in bitches after whelping. The nursing mum will run a temperature, be off her food and generally not feel well. The discharge from her vulva will be brown, thick and smelly. Her womb is infected and she needs immediate veterinary attention. Bitches can have metritis at other times, usually just after their season. Those afflicted are often elderly. Symptoms are excessive drinking, possible vomiting, and perhaps a nasty discharge from the vulva. She will show signs of feeling unwell. The veterinary surgeon may treat her with antibiotics but will probably operate to remove her womb.

Bloat. Or more correctly gastric dilation is a condition to which Irish Setters are susceptible. For some unknown reason food begins to ferment in the stomach and the dog seems to be unable to 'belch' up the rapidly forming gases. The dog makes continued gulping movements and half-heartedly tries to be sick. It is very restless and cannot lie comfortably on its side. The abdomen becomes very badly distended and will sound as a big bass drum if gently tapped with the fingers. This is a very vicious condition causing rapid severe shock and a painful death and needs immediate veterinary treatment. One traditional recommendation – to avoid bloat – is never exercise a dog on a full stomach.

Veterinary Surgeon

Anyone owning a dog should have a veterinary surgeon – and both sides have a hand in making it a successful relationship. To start with, make a note of his consulting hours and telephone number. Many people have access to several possible vets and they should choose one they will get on with. It is unfair to everyone if they persist with a veterinary surgeon they dislike. If there is dissatisfaction over recommended treatment or the results of treatment on a particular occasion, then politely ask for a second opinion. Angry words and a speedy switch to another veterinary practice may prove embarrassing. The first veterinary surgeon may have been right and, even worse, preferable to the one you ran to. Re-crossing burnt bridges can be difficult.

Old age

This is an anxious time for a devoted owner, as the old dog is obviously more susceptible to ills and chills. A Setter stays young a long time and continues to be very active until around ten years old. Though he will start to take things easy, he will continue to enjoy his daily walks, trotting rather than galloping. Of course, there are exceptions to this rule as dogs are like people and a terminal disease or accident can alter the normal course of events. The average life span of a Setter is around twelve years. It can vary from nine to fifteen. Bitches often live longer than dogs.

Cosset the old Irish a little and give him a warm cosy bed and perhaps a coat to wear on very cold days. He may have a delicate digestion so give him two small meals per day. Let him get up late in the morning – he's probably a little creaky with rheumatism and moves slowly to start off – and go to bed when he feels like it.

Teeth can be a problem. Tartar makes them loose and they can go bad and make his breath offensive. It is a good idea to have them cleaned and the loose or bad ones removed under anaesthetic before he is too old for such a risk. Dogs manage very well with fewer teeth and continue to enjoy their food.

Various ailments occur in old age, so be on the watch for any symptoms.

Rheumatism or arthritis often trouble the oldie but the veterinary surgeon can help here.

The heart sometimes becomes dicky: watch out for fast breathing and a dry cough. Fluid in the lungs often goes with a bad heart. Your veterinary surgeon can prescribe various pills for a while longer, all being well.

Excessive thirst can be a symptom of kidney disease, metritis or diabetes, so get the complaint diagnosed quickly. One of my bitches in her ninth year developed diabetes and following an operation for metritis she seemed to have given up the ghost. Nothing would tempt her. And then we had a brainwave. She was a most maternal bitch, so we slipped into the nursery and returned with a four-day-old Cavalier King Charles spaniel pup. Her nose twitched, her eyes flickered and showed interest . . . and she never looked back, eventually throwing off all traces of diabetes and returning to her old, happy self.

However, the time will come when the old dog will find life a burden and cannot enjoy it any more. The kindest thing to do is have your veterinary surgeon come to the house, and administer the final injection to your old friend while he lies placidly in your arms. His last few moments will thus be happy ones. Although it is very hard for you, he deserves this last consideration.

APPENDIX A

Annual Registrations at the Kennel Club: 1940 to 1980

1940	331	1954	447	1968	1983
1941	195	1955	506	1969	2679
1942	330	1956	384	1970	3277
1943	579	1957	461	1971	3764
1944	947	1958	461	1972	4792
1945	1214	1959	513	1973	5438
1946	1748	1960	496	1974	5590
1947	1372	1961	497	1975	4898
1948	1111	1962	660	1976	2198
1949	1069	1963	712	1977	1244
1950	913	1964	758	1978	3228
1951	774	1965	962	1979	5190
1952	527	1966	1200	1980	4779
1953	462	1967	1458		

APPENDIX B

Breed Clubs

Irish Setter Association (England)
Irish Setter Breeders Club
Irish Setter Club of Scotland
Irish Setter Club of Wales
Belfast and District Irish Setter Club
Setter and Pointer Club
South of England Irish Setter Club
The North East of England Irish Setter Club

The names and addresses of secretaries can be obtained on application to the Kennel Club, 1 Clarges Street, London, W1Y 8AB

APPENDIX C

Pedigrees of Key Dogs

Sh. Ch. Brackenfield Hartsbourne Bronze
Brackenfield Dandelion
Sh. Ch. Raycroft Hoobram Rich Corona
Ch. Gaelge Ardrew Pride
Sh. Ch. Marrona Marica
Sh. Ch. Wendover Gentleman
- Watendlath Double Top
- Victory of Mearnesse
- Beau of Wendover
- Beorcham Miss Bracken
- Beorcham Blases of Wendover
- Wendover Bracken
- Pensive Patrick
- Delia of Wendover

SH. CH. BRACKENFIELD HARTSBOURNE BRONZE

Parent	*Grand-Parents*	*G.G.-Parents*	*G.G.G.-Parents*
Am. Ch. and Sh. Ch. Hartsbourne Brilliant	Sh. Ch. Hartsbourne Tobias	Hartsbourne Masterstroke	Hartsbourne Masterpiece
			Hartsbourne Purros Zoe
		Hartsbourne Flame	Ir. Ch. Brilliant Bob
			Derrybrien Sally
	Ch. Hartsbourne Popsy	Hartsbourne Senor of Shadowood (Am. Import)	Am. Ch. Coppe
			of Crosshaven
			Queen of Ardkeen's Moll
		Hartsbourne Poppet	Hartsbourne Masterpiece
			Susan of Besandus
Hartsbourne Purros Petula	Ricardero Padriac of Silverglade	Beau of Wendover	Ir. Ch. Kerry o Wendover
			Beorcham Bracken
		Berclarhan Macushla	Hartsbourne Masterpiece
			Sadie of Bickenhall
	Hartsbourne Clodagh	Ch. Padriac of Matsonhouse	Ch. Grellan of Matsonhouse
			Sh. Ch. Nutbro Sherry
		Hartsbourne Truthful	Ch. Borrowdale Tristan
			Ch. Hartsbourn Veracity

BRACKENFIELD DANDELION

	Grand-Parents	*G.G.-Parents*	*G.G.G.-Parents*
:h. and ı. Erinhaven s Muldoon Import)	Trottwood Tristan	Am. Ch. Thenderin Brian Tristan	Am. Ch. End O'Maine Luckalone
			Am. Ch. Kinvarra Portia
		Trottwood Dawnadere	Am. Ch. Brian of Tyrone
			Am. Ch. Oakley Dawnadere
	Knightscroft Kerry Dancer	Knightscroft Marty Muldoon	Am. Ch. Milson O'Boy II
			Jordan Farm Scarlett O'Hara
		Am. Ch. Knightscroft Dark Susanne	Knightscroft Terence
			Knightscroft Lucky Penny
enfield	Brynmount Redgaynes Mars	Rheola Bendickon	Rheola Benedict
			Corbie
		Brynmount Sheilamhor	Shaun of Sheringham
			Cuailgne Ceilidhe Mhor
	Smallbridge Poppy	Sh. Ch. Storm of Casamia	Beau of Wendover
			Lady Casamia
		Raycroft Meg	Sh. Ch. Raycroft Mediator
			Raycroft Scarlet

SH. CH. RAYCROFT HOOBRAM RICH CORONA

Parents	*Grand-Parents*	*G.G.-Parents*	*G.G.G.-Parents*
Sh. Ch. Raycroft Pirate	Sh. Ch. Raycroft Rowdy	Sh. Ch. Hartsbourne O'Hara	Sh. Ch. Hartsbourne T
			Hartsbourne Popsy
		Ch. Raycroft Rena	Sh. Ch. Raycro Mediator
			Derrycarne Redwine
	Ch. Raycroft Hartsbourne Perdita	Sh. Ch. Hartsbourne Tobias	Hartsbourne Masterstroke
			Hartsbourne Flame
		Hartsbourne Purros Petula	Ricardero Padri of Silverglade
			Hartsbourne Clodagh
Tesa of Ballyrobyn	Ch. Gaelge Ardrew Pride	Ch. Gaelge Copperplate of Ide	Branscombe Robyn
			Sh. Ch. Ronor Rena of Ide
		Peacemakers Charming	Peacemaker of Glyncoed
			Pevrill of Glyncoed
	Jane of Ballyrobyn	Magwills Bawddwr Pride	Ch. Gaelge Copperplate of Ide
			Bawddwr Lass
		Newrath Lass	Robin Amour
			Othene Beauty

CH. GAELGE ARDREW PRIDE

ent	*Grand-Parents*	*G.G.-Parents*	*G.G.G.-Parents*
Gaelge pperplate de	Branscombe Robyn	Hartsbourne Shaun	Ch. Padriac of Matsonhouse
			Kotuko of Quiquern
		Norlan Golden Girl	Norlan Michael
			Norlan Sheila
	Sh. Ch. Ronor Rena of Ide	Ronor Rory	Rex
			Miss Rufus of Ormeau
		Ronor Rachel	Rusty
			Sheila
cemakers rming	Peacemaker of Glyncoed	Pegomas of Glyncoed	Ch. Son of a Gun of Gadeland
			Prudence of Glyncoed
		Petal of Glyncoed	Pirate of Glyncoed
			Hollywood Pride
	Pevrill of Glyncoed	Pilot of Glyncoed	Pirate of Glyncoed
			Hollywood Pride
		Mintymona of Glyncoed	Ch. Son of a Gun of Gladeland
			Mintytoo

SH. CH. MARRONA MARICA

Parents	*Grand-Parents*	*G.G.-Parents*	*G.G.G.-Parents*
Sh. Ch. Norlan Paddy	Sh. Ch. Watendlath Kevin O'Pandy	Victory Moon	Pensive Patrick
			Delia of Wendover
		Watendlath Jael O'Pandy	Watendlath Double Top
			Victory of Mearnesse
	Norlan Odette of Oosh	Sh. Ch. Hartsbourne O'Hara	Sh. Ch. Hartsbourne Tc
			Ch. Hartsbourn Popsy
		Paprika of Oosh	Shandy of Maydorwill
			Sallyann of Oosh
Sh. Ch. Marrona Merope	Marrona Milesian	Watendlath João O'Pandy	Watendlath Double Top
			Victory of Mearnesse
		Wendover Witchery	Beau of Wendover
			Beorcham Miss Bracken
	Flicka of Casamia	Sh. Ch. Hartsbourne Brilliant	Sh. Ch. Hartsbourne Tc
			Ch. Hartsbourn Popsy
		Melody of Casamia	Sh. Ch. Bracke Romulus of Cas
			Sh. Ch. Gail of Casamia

SH. CH. WENDOVER GENTLEMAN

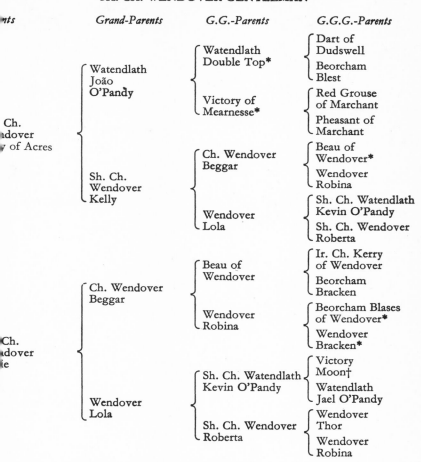

nts	*Grand-Parents*	*G.G.-Parents*	*G.G.G.-Parents*
Ch. ndover y of Acres	Watendlath João O'Pandy	Watendlath Double Top*	Dart of Dudswell
			Beorcham Blest
		Victory of Mearnesse*	Red Grouse of Marchant
			Pheasant of Marchant
	Sh. Ch. Wendover Kelly	Ch. Wendover Beggar	Beau of Wendover*
			Wendover Robina
		Wendover Lola	Sh. Ch. Watendlath Kevin O'Pandy
			Sh. Ch. Wendover Roberta
Ch. ndover ie	Ch. Wendover Beggar	Beau of Wendover	Ir. Ch. Kerry of Wendover
			Beorcham Bracken
		Wendover Robina	Beorcham Blases of Wendover*
			Wendover Bracken*
	Wendover Lola	Sh. Ch. Watendlath Kevin O'Pandy	Victory Moon†
			Watendlath Jael O'Pandy
		Sh. Ch. Wendover Roberta	Wendover Thor
			Wendover Robina

following pages for extension of one parent's pedigree
following pages for extension of two parents' pedigrees

WATENDLATH DOUBLE TOP

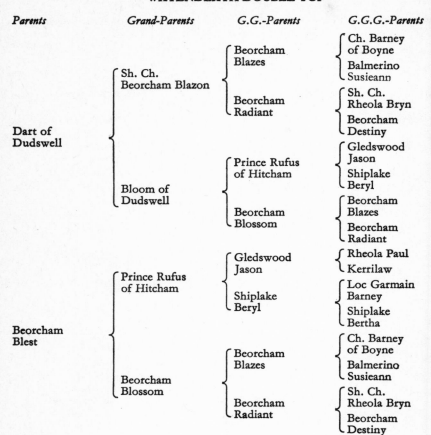

Parents	*Grand-Parents*	*G.G.-Parents*	*G.G.G.-Parents*
Dart of Dudswell	Sh. Ch. Beorcham Blazon	Beorcham Blazes	Ch. Barney of Boyne
			Balmerino Susieann
		Beorcham Radiant	Sh. Ch. Rheola Bryn
			Beorcham Destiny
	Bloom of Dudswell	Prince Rufus of Hitcham	Gledswood Jason
			Shiplake Beryl
		Beorcham Blossom	Beorcham Blazes
			Beorcham Radiant
Beorcham Blest	Prince Rufus of Hitcham	Gledswood Jason	Rheola Paul
			Kerrilaw
		Shiplake Beryl	Loc Garmain Barney
			Shiplake Bertha
	Beorcham Blossom	Beorcham Blazes	Ch. Barney of Boyne
			Balmerino Susieann
		Beorcham Radiant	Sh. Ch. Rheola Bryn
			Beorcham Destiny

VICTORY OF MEARNESSE

rents	*Grand-Parents*	*G.G.-Parents*	*G.G.G.-Parents*
ed Grouse Marchant	Rufus of Thurston	Wag of Wendover	Rheola Benedict
			Rona of Wendover
		Delia of Wendover	Ch. Portlairge Steady of Wendover
			Crimson Vamp
	Sayla of Bickenhall	Slick of Ide	Sir Patrick of Clodagh
			Security of Buntingford
		Firefly of Bickenhall	Sportsman of Gadeland
			Bickenhall Gadfly
easant of rchant	Rufus of Thurston	Wag of Wendover	Rheola Benedict
			Rona of Wendover
		Delia of Wendover	Ch. Portlairge Steady of Wendover
			Crimson Vamp
	Lassie of Craigburn	Brofurn Barney	Ch. Menaifron Pat O'Moy
			Brofurn Bridget
		Brofurn Brynk	Borrowdale Jake
			Brofurn Berenice

BEAU OF WENDOVER

Parents	*Grand-Parents*	*G.G.-Parents*	*G.G.G.-Parents*
Ir. Ch. Kerry of Wendover	Ch. Padriac of Matsonhouse	Ch. Grellan of Matsonhouse	Sh. Ch. Shaun of Matsonhouse
			Corbie
		Nutbrown Sherry	US Ch. Golden Dawn of Gadelan
			Nutbrown Tessa
	Cleo	Gift of Gadeland	Ch. Son of a Gun of Gadeland
			Collett O'Connell
		Brandy of Llantarnum	Danny O'Moy
			Pandora of Elmford
Beorcham Bracken	Beorcham Blazes	Ch. Barney of Boyne	Donnie Rhu
			Ch. Oonagh of Boyne
		Beorcham Radiant	Sh. Ch. Rheola Bryn
			Beorcham Destiny
	Rinda of Dendy	Sh. Ch. Shamus of Ballyshannon	Sh. Ch. Rheola Bryn
			Cloud of Silverlands
		Candy Tuft	Wizbang Buccaneer
			Lady at Law

BEORCHAM MISS BRACKEN

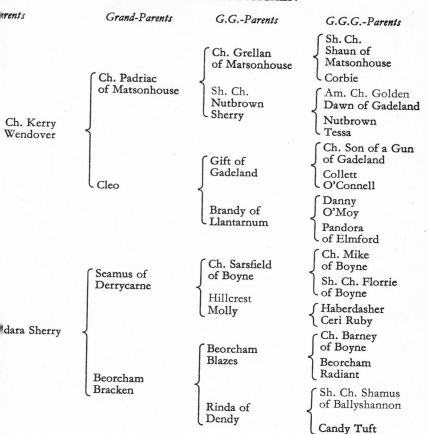

rents	*Grand-Parents*	*G.G.-Parents*	*G.G.G.-Parents*
Ch. Kerry Wendover	Ch. Padriac of Matsonhouse	Ch. Grellan of Matsonhouse	Sh. Ch. Shaun of Matsonhouse
			Corbie
		Sh. Ch. Nutbrown Sherry	Am. Ch. Golden Dawn of Gadeland
			Nutbrown Tessa
	Cleo	Gift of Gadeland	Ch. Son of a Gun of Gadeland
			Collett O'Connell
		Brandy of Llantarnum	Danny O'Moy
			Pandora of Elmford
dara Sherry	Seamus of Derrycarne	Ch. Sarsfield of Boyne	Ch. Mike of Boyne
			Sh. Ch. Florrie of Boyne
		Hillcrest Molly	Haberdasher
			Ceri Ruby
	Beorcham Bracken	Beorcham Blazes	Ch. Barney of Boyne
			Beorcham Radiant
		Rinda of Dendy	Sh. Ch. Shamus of Ballyshannon
			Candy Tuft

BEORCHAM BLASES OF WENDOVER

Parents	*Grand-Parents*	*G.G.-Parents*	*G.G.G.-Parents*
Sh. Ch. Beorcham Blazon	Beorcham Blazes	Ch. Barney of Boyne	Donnie Rhu
			Ch. Oonagh of Boyne
		Balmerino Susieann	Dermot The Pride
			Bryn Awel Blissfull
	Beorcham Radiant	Sh. Ch. Rheola Bryn	Don Sancho
			Sh. Ch. Rheola Didona
		Beorcham Destiny	Ben d'Or
			Beorcham Clarin
Beorcham Miss Bracken	Ir. Ch. Kerry of Wendover	Ch. Padriac of Matsonhouse	Ch. Grellan of Matsonhouse
			Sh. Ch. Nutbrow Sherry
		Cleo	Gift of Gadeland
			Brandy of Llantarnum
	Cilldara Sherry	Seamus of Derrycarne	Ch. Sarsfield of Boyne
			Hillcrest Molly
		Beorcham Bracken	Beorcham Blazes
			Rinda of Dendy

WENDOVER BRACKEN

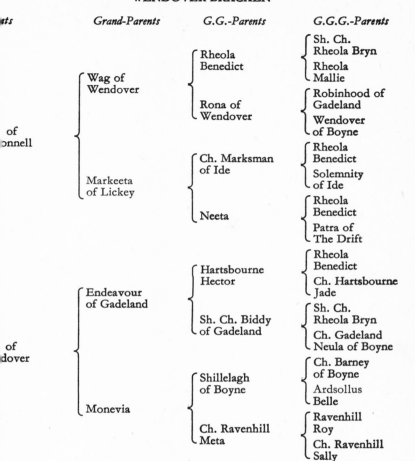

ts	*Grand-Parents*	*G.G.-Parents*	*G.G.G.-Parents*
of onnell	Wag of Wendover	Rheola Benedict	Sh. Ch. Rheola Bryn
			Rheola Mallie
		Rona of Wendover	Robinhood of Gadeland
			Wendover of Boyne
	Markeeta of Lickey	Ch. Marksman of Ide	Rheola Benedict
			Solemnity of Ide
		Neeta	Rheola Benedict
			Patra of The Drift
of dover	Endeavour of Gadeland	Hartsbourne Hector	Rheola Benedict
			Ch. Hartsbourne Jade
		Sh. Ch. Biddy of Gadeland	Sh. Ch. Rheola Bryn
			Ch. Gadeland Neula of Boyne
	Monevia	Shillelagh of Boyne	Ch. Barney of Boyne
			Ardsollus Belle
		Ch. Ravenhill Meta	Ravenhill Roy
			Ch. Ravenhill Sally

PENSIVE PATRICK

(Sire of Victory Moon, who is sire of Sh. Ch. Watendlath Kevin O'Pandy)

Parents	*Grand-Parents*	*G.G.-Parents*	*G.G.G.-Parents*
Wag of Wendover	Rheola Benedict	Sh. Ch. Rheola Bryn	Don Sancho
			Sh. Ch. Rheola Didona
		Rheola Mallie	Prince Plastine
			Rheola Bertha
	Rona of Wendover	Robin Hood of Gadeland	Rheola Boniface
			Sh. Ch. Biddy of Gadeland
		Wendover of Boyne	Ch. Barney of Boyne
			Sh. Ch. Florrie of Boyne
Miranda Maid	Ch. Sarsfield of Boyne	Ch. Mike of Boyne	Demon of Boyne
			Malva of Boyne
		Sh. Ch. Florrie of Boyne	Ch. Terry of Boyne
			Ch. Ravenhill Sally
	Lady Peg	Kyrewood Rambler	Mike of Carminowe
			Kyre Linnet
		Shiplake Tessa of Kyrewood	Loc Garmain Barney
			Watermill Brenda

DELIA OF WENDOVER
(Dam of Victory Moon, who is sire of Sh. Ch. Watendlath Kevin O'Pandy)

ts	*Grand-Parents*	*G.G.-Parents*	*G.G.G.-Parents*
ortlairge y of lover	Coileac	Ir. FT Ch. Eilteog	Ch. Gruagach
			Oona of Derrynane
		Ir. Ch. Maisie of Charleville	Pride of Castlewrixon
			Castlewrixon Belle
	Doobin Queen	FT Ch. Rhu Gorse	Gorse of Auburn
			Rubra
		Unshinagh Nellie	Abercorn Pest
			Greencastle Sensation
on Vamp	Robin Hood of Gadeland	Rheola Boniface	Sh. Ch. Rheola Bryn
			Rheola Mallie
		Sh. Ch. Biddy of Gadeland	Sh. Ch. Rheola Bryn
			Ch. Gadeland Neula of Boyne
	Sally of Rivermead	Wendover Wizard	Ch. Sarsfield of Boyne
			Deirdre of Boyne
		Paramount Sally	Loc Garmain Don
			Moira Macfin

APPENDIX D

Champions 1960–1980

All dogs not listed as Ch. or FT Ch. are Sh. Ch.

Name	Sex	Birth	Sire	Dam	Breeder	Owner
1960 Ch. Boisdale Boggit	D	26–5–55	Wendover Bosun	Boisdale Solitaire	Owner	Mrs M. C. Darling
Forestred Rodney	D	10–8–55	Ch. Brackenfield Hartsbourne Bronze	Brackenfield Petal	Mrs B. G. Griffin	Mr E. C. Payne
Hartsbourne O'Kelly	D	30–3–58	Sh. Ch. Hartsbourne O'Mara	Sh. Ch. Hartsbourne Honeysuckle	Owner	Mrs E. K. Walker
Loongana Red Biddy of Portarlie	B	11–3–58	Ir. Ch. Cuanhills Calling	Loongana Tosca of Portarlie	Mrs D. Mateer	Mrs E. K. Scott-Gentles
Wendover Katie	B	6–4–58	Ch. Wendover Beggar	Wendover Lola	Owner	Mr and Mrs L. C. James
1961 FT Ch. Sulhamstead Nearco d'Or	D	11–5–57	Sulhamstead Bristle d'Or	FT Ch. Sulhamstead Nina d'Or	Owners	Mrs F. Nagle and Miss M. Clark
FT Ch. Sulhamstead Nibs d'Or	D	26–11–57	FT Ch. Sulhamstead Basil d'Or	FT Ch. Sulhamstead Nina d'Or	Owners	Mrs F. Nagle and Miss M. Clark
Wendover Castor	D	23–5–57	Eamon of Casamia	Sh. Ch.	Mr and Mrs L. C.	Mr and Mrs C. T.

Giselle of Oosh	B	16–1–55	Sh. Ch. Hartsbourne O'Hara	Paprika of Oosh	Mrs A. J. Leighton-Boyce	Mrs E. Laughton Moore
Hartsbourne Tulip	B	30–3–58	Sh. Ch. Hartsbourne O'Mara	Sh. Ch. Hartsbourne Honeysuckle	Owner	Mrs E. K. Walker
FT Ch. Moylrath Blaze	B	23–10–57	Portown Romeo	Red Blaze	Mr J. Ryan	Mr P. Bradley
FT Ch. Tullyelmer Lark	B	7–1–57	Grouse Hall	Ruby of Mount Eagle	Mr P. J. O'Connell	Col A. C. Moore
Wendover Romance	B	2–4–56	Watendlath João O'Pandy	Sh. Ch. Wendover Roberta	Mr and Mrs L. C. James	Miss J. Russell
1962 Brackenfield Elm	D	3–11–58	Ch. Brackenfield Hartsbourne Bronze	Brackenfield Holly	Mr and Mrs R. Cordwell	Mr R. Cordwell
Norlan Paddy	D	20–6–57	Sh. Ch. Watendlath Kevin O'Pandy	Norlan Odette of Oosh	Mrs E. F. Leighton-Boyce	Miss N. Tomlison
Raycroft Hoobram Rich Corona	D	23–12–59	Sh. Ch. Raycroft Pirate	Tesa of Ballyrobyn	J. A. Greenwood	Mr and Mrs C. Furness
Gaelge Gertina	B	3–5–56	Ch. Wendover Beggar	Gaelge Griselda	Owner	Mr J. Whittaker
Marrona Merope	B	1–9–58	Marrona Milesian	Flicka of Casamia	Owner	Mrs M. E. Stokes
FT Ch. Rahard Belle	B	15–2–56	Portown Romeo	Red Blaze	Mr J. Ryan	Mr P. F. Goodwin
Wonderful of Acres	B	16–7–59	Wendover Shandy of Casamia	Wondermark of Acres	Owner	Miss B. Pruddah

Name	*Sex*	*Birth*	*Sire*	*Dam*	*Breeder*	*Owner*
1963 Brendower Bounty	D	13-5-60	Brenhow Gay Gavin	Brackenfield Wallflower	Owner	Mrs B. M. Howe
Brackenfield Lozell Whisper	B	21-12-58	Ch. Brackenfield Hartsbourne Bronze	Flicka of Lozell	Mrs G. F. Hollington	Miss S. J. Lennox
Gaelge Gisena	B	6-7-61	Sh. Ch. Raycroft Hoobram Rich Corona	Sh. Ch. Gaelge Gertina	Owner	Mr J. Whittaker
Raycroft Bramble	B	20-4-58	Ch. Wendover Beggar	Raycroft Primrose	Owner	Mr and Mrs C. E. Furness
Wendover Kelly	B	6-4-58	Ch. Wendover Beggar	Wendover Lola	Owner	Mr and Mrs L. C. James
1964 FT Ch. Ballymac Eagle	D	26-3-59	Prince of Kilmurray	Currow Gem	Mr S. Dennehy	Rev. A. S. Connor
Heathcliffe Jason	D	23-2-61	Brackenfield Dandelion	Heathcliffe Portia	Mrs A. Butler	Miss P. Taylor and B. Worth
Wendover Vagabond	D	20-3-61	Ch. Wendover Beggar	Wendover Lola	Owner	Mr and Mrs L. C. James
Brackenfield May	B	1-9-62	Brackenfield Dandelion	Brackenfield Viola	Owner	Miss S. J. Lennox
Hartsbourne Zinnia	B	20-4-61	Sh. Ch. Hartsbourne O'Mara	Sh. Ch. Hartsbourne Honeysuckle	Owner	Mrs E. K. Walker
Raycroft Tammie	B	6-7-61	Sh. Ch. Raycroft [illegible]	Sh. Ch. Gaelge [illegible]	Mr J. Whittaker	Mr and Mrs C. E. [illegible]

[illegible] Minny	D	[illegible]	[illegible] Moan-ruad Admiral	[illegible] Belle	Mr F. F. Goodwin	Mr R. A. Stewart
1965 Cornevon Snowstorm	D	28–1–63	Cornevon Coppernob	Brackenfield Iris	Owner	Mrs A. M. and Miss J. M. Gibson
Gaelge Gisela	B	11–3–60	Gaelge Garson	Sh. Ch. Gaelge Gertina	Owner	Mr J. Whittaker
Wendover Nancy	B	8–6–62	NZ Ch. Wendover Gary of Acres	Sh. Ch. Wendover Katie	Owner	Mr and Mrs L. C. James
1966 Hartsbourne Heron	D	8–8–63	Sh. Ch. Raycroft Hoobram Rich Corona	Sh. Ch. Hartsbourne Tulip	Owner	Mrs E. K. Walker
Ch. Kinsman of Chatham	D	31–3–61	Trottwood	Radiance of Springcroft	Mr and Mrs I. M. Wise	Mr S. V. Foy
Raycroft Call Boy	D	27–11–63	Hartsbourne Kerry	Sh. Ch. Raycroft Bramble	Mr and Miss C. Furness	Mrs C. Furness
Marrona Marica	B	27–9–60	Sh. Ch. Norlan Paddy	Sh. Ch. Marrona Merope	Mrs M. E. Stokes	Mr and Mrs D. J. Stephens
Wendover Brulette	B	7–6–63	Sh. Ch. Wendover Vagabond	Sh. Ch. Wendover Romance	Miss J. Russell	Mr and Mrs L. C. James
1967 Bidford Buffin	D	22–6–62	Ch. Wendover Beggar	Sh. Ch. Marrona Marica	Owner	Mr and Mrs D. J. Stephens
Wendover Gentleman	D	8–6–62	NZ Ch. Wendover Gary of Acres	Sh. Ch. Wendover Katie	Owner	Mr and Mrs L. C. James

Name	*Sex*	*Birth*	*Sire*	*Dam*	*Breeder*	*Owner*
Joanma's Lottie	B	18–6–64	Wendover Game	Wendover Kara	Owner	Mrs S. Culpin
Vandamist Vision	B	3–6–62	Marrona Midas of Vandamist	Sowerhill Red Mist	Owner	Mrs E. G. Thompson
Ch. Wendover Romance	B	FT qualifying certificate (See 1961 for details)				
1968 FT Ch. Ridgetor Firbanks	D	12–5–65	Ridgetor Pawnee	Viana Red Suzanne	Mr D. E. Wannop	Dr J. M. Beazley
Scotswood Barabbas	D	19–3–66	Wendover Game	Scotswood Hot Sensation	Owner	Mrs R. Bryden
Wendover Ballymoss	D	7–6–63	Sh. Ch. Wendover Vagabond	Sh. Ch. Wendover Romance	Miss J. Russell	Mr and Mrs L. C. James
Marrona Marigold of Thurnbrook	B	27–9–60	Sh. Ch. Norlan Paddy	Sh. Ch. Marrona Merope	Mrs M. E. Stokes	Mrs J. C. Parsons
Morningstar Melanie	B	3–8–63	Gormac Morning Sunrise	Lady Jane of Cooksey	Mr and Mrs Woodward	Mrs B. Birch
FT Ch. and Ir. FT Ch. Patricia of Killone	B	22–4–62	Waydown Sandy	FT Ch. and Ir. FT Ch. Rahard Belle	Mr P. Goodwin	Mr J. Nash
Raycroft Chorus Girl	B	20–8–65	Sh. Ch. Raycroft Callboy	Sh. Ch. Raycroft Tammie	Mrs C. E. Furness	Miss V. Thorne Baker
Wendover Katrina	B	1–3–63	Sh. Ch. Wendover Vagabond	Cherry Wonder	Mr Powell	Mr and Mrs L. C. James

1969 Brackenfield Orichalc Juniper	D	23–2–65	Ch. Brackenfield Hartsbourne Bronze	Orichalc Freyja	Mrs V. Page	Miss S. J. Lennox
Brackenfield Tertius	D	11–6–66	Ch. Brackenfield Orichalc Juniper	Sh. Ch. Brackenfield Lozell Whisper	Owner	Miss S. J. Lennox
Brendower Bomber	D	13–5–60	Brenhow Gay Gavin	Brackenfield Wallflower	Mrs B. M. Howe	Mrs D. L. Parry
Cornevon Prince Charming	D	2–1–66	Wendover Game	Cornevon Snowbunting	Owner and Mrs A. Gibson	Mrs J. M. Roberts
Wendover Caskey	D	14–10–65	Sh. Ch. Wendover Vagabond	Wendover Sorrel	Miss C. Beresford	Mrs C. Heron
Bronte of Castleoak	B	25–6–64	Gaelge Gaffer	Jessica of Castleoak	Mr and Mrs P. Davis	Mrs L. M. Davis
Cornevon Cinderella	B	2–1–66	Wendover Game	Cornevon Snowbunting	Owner and Mrs A. Gibson	Mrs J. M. Roberts
FT Ch. Divis Gem	B	10–3–66	Slievebawn Captain	Gay Red Stella	Mr R. Law	Mr K. Patterson
Fearnley Firecracker	B	4–4–65	Ryan O'Rafferty	Wendover Bronze	Mr M. Harley	Mr and Mrs B. F. Rhodes
Hartsbourne Starlight	B	18–1–66	Hartsbourne Comet	Sh. Ch. Hartsbourne Zinnia	Owner	Mrs E. K. Walker
1970 Ch. Brackenfield Orichalc Juniper		FT qualifying certificate (See 1969 for details)				
Twoacres Troilus	D	2–1–68	Sh. Ch. Wendover Gentleman	Musbury Melisande of Twoacres	Owner	Mrs J. C. Coates

Name	*Sex*	*Birth*	*Sire*	*Dam*	*Breeder*	*Owner*
Wendover Royalist	D	13–3–67	Sh. Ch. Wendover Ballymoss	Sh. Ch. Wendover Kelly	Owner	Mr and Mrs L. C. James
FT Ch. & Ir. FT Ch. Bena of Maytown	B	5–3–64	FT Ch. & Ir. FT Ch. Ballymac Eagle	Shelia of Moanruad	Rev. A. O'Connor	Mr J. Nash
Cherrybeech Sabrina	B	3–10–66	Raycroft Larry	Vandamist Vanessa	Mrs J. Goldsworthy	Mr and Mrs L. R. Powers
Cherrybeech Vandamist Bronze Velvet	B	18–3–65	Rychma Rouge	Cherrybeech Enchantress of Vandamist	Mrs E. Thompson	Mrs J. Goldsworthy
Cornevon Primrose	B	10–2–68	Sh. Ch. Scotswood Barabbas	Cornevon Snowbunting	Owner	Mrs J. M. Roberts
FT Ch. Danske Moymore Lulu	B	11–4–67	FT Ch. & Ir. FT Ch. Ballymac Eagle	Danske Ballinard Miss of Annagh	Mrs W. Wheeler	Miss M. C. Aitken
Loongana Lough Sheelin	B	24–3–65	Hartsbourne Cashel	Loongana Magic Moments	Owner	Mrs D. Mateer
Timadon Ballywestow Festoon	B	18–8–66	Sh. Ch. Wendover Vagabond	Ch. Wendover Romance	Miss J. Russell	Mr G. Coupe
1971 Carnbargus Hartsbourne O'Brady	D	15–6–66	Hartsbourne O'Keefe	Hartsbourne Hydrangea	Mrs E. Walker	Mrs E. Gardner
Chestnut of Wellbeck	D	5–10–66	Wendover Fred	Bidford Babette	Mr and Mrs C. H. Tallis	Mr and Mrs R. S. Burns
Ch. Joanma's Adriano	D	20–3–65	Wendover Game	Copper Retford	Mrs R. Silverman	Mr P. A. Heard

Twoacres Tamburlaine	D	2–1–68	Sh. Ch. Wendover Gentleman	Musbury Melisande of Twoacres	Mrs J. Coates	Miss P. Scott
Cornevon Violet	B	10–2–68	Sh. Ch. Scotswood Barabbas	Cornevon Snowbunting	Owner	Mrs J. M. Roberts
Hartsbourne Astra	B	18–1–66	Hartsbourne Comet	Sh. Ch. Hartsbourne Zinnia	Mrs E. Walker	Miss V. A. Albertis
Twoacres Teresa	B	2–1–68	Sh. Ch. Wendover Gentleman	Musbury Melisande of Twoacres	Mrs J. Coates	Mrs S. Whittaker
Twoacres Traviata	B	2–1–68	Sh. Ch. Wendover Gentleman	Musbury Melisande of Twoacres	Mrs J. Coates	Mrs J. Quinn
1972 Corriecas Baron	D	14–2–69	Sh. Ch. Wendover Gentleman	Corriecas Sheba	Owner	Mrs B. Levick
FT Ch. Grouse of Maytown	D	6–9–68	Eng. and Ir. FT Ch. Ballymac Eagle	Flyaway Kay	Rev. O.Connor	Mr R. M. McElhinney
Hurricane of Carramore	D	20–1–69	Sh. Ch. Scotswood Barabbas	Kathryn Rhu of Carramore	Owner	Mrs M. Hurll
Joanma's Saffron	D	28–1–70	Joanma's Don	Wendover Chell	Mrs Eckersley	Mrs M. Jarosz
Flame of Allsquare	B	19–11–66	Brackenfield Dandelion	Brackenfield Wistful	Owner	Mr J. M. Johnson
Sowerhill Red Colleen of Kitewood	B	10–12–68	Sh. Ch. Wendover Gentleman	Morning Mist of Andana	Mrs T. Penny	Miss O. M. Hunt
Wendover Hussy	B	10–6–67	Sh. Ch. Wendover Gentleman	Wendover Jana	Owner	Mr and Mrs L. C. James

Name	Sex	Birth	Sire	Dam	Breeder	Owner
1973						
FT Ch. Cleo of Maytown	D	1–4–67	FT Ch. Ballymac Eagle	Flyaway Kay	Owner	Rev. O'Connor
Cornevon Lovebird	D	14–1–71	Sh. Ch. Cornevon Prince Charming	Sh. Ch. Cornevon Primrose	Mrs J. M. Roberts	Mr J. A. Watt
Monty Count of Medena	D	4–10–69	Channel Marabout Monty	Bideawhile Brilliant	Mr D. Harris	Miss M. A. Lowell
Wendover Herald of Cuprea	D	8–2–70	Sh. Ch. Wendover Gentleman	Gaelge Gariona	Mr G. Coupe	Mr and Mrs F. A. Fanning
Wendover Highlander	D	24–4–70	Sh. Ch. Wendover Royalist	Ruani Redhead	Miss C. Besford	Mr and Mrs L. C. James
Wendover Racketeer	D	27–5–69	Sh. Ch. Wendover Vagabond	Wendover Humorist	Owner	Mr and Mrs L. C. James
Brackenfield Verbena	B	21–11–70	Sh. Ch. Hartsbourne Trident	Sh. Ch. Brackenfield May	Owner	Miss S. Lennox
Emmafield Aubanjon Adventuress	B	22–12–69	Moval Red Warrior	Marshlea Merry Marrie	Mr A. Petty	Mrs J. M. Aspinell
Greenglades Golden Dream	B	20–4–69	Sh. Ch. Brackenfield Tertius	Sh. Ch. Hartsbourne Astra	Owner	Miss V. A. Albertis
Melony Minet	B	8–12–68	Ch. Brackenfield Orichalc Juniper	Halstock Rosina	Owner	Mrs G. G. Follows
Rickerscot Bridget Maguire	B	18–8–69	Sh. Ch. Scotswood Barabbas	Rickerscot Clover Colleen	Mr and Mrs S. A. Briggs	Mrs B. Birch
Wendover Lady May	B	24–3–69	Sh. Ch. Wendover Ballymoss	Wendover Change	Mr and Mrs L. C. James	Mrs K. and Miss J. Norman

1974 Barnsforde Winston	D	9–3–72	Sh. Ch. Hartsbourne Trident	Vanity of Barnsforde	Owner	Mr and Mrs A. Dodman
Hartsbourne Trident	D	19–6–67	Sh. Ch. Brackenfield Tertius	Hartsbourne Velvet	Mrs E. K. Walker	Miss S. Lennox
Margretwoods Craftsman	D	11–4–70	Sh. Ch. Scotswood Barabbas	Bridget of Castleoak	Owner	Mrs S. B. Neave
Stephenshill Gamebird	D	12–3–71	Lenwyn Gamecock	Duchess of Bickenhall	Owner	Mr N. W. Morrish
Timadon Kendel	D	17–3–70	Sh. Ch. Wendover Royalist	Timadon Dorianne	Owner	Mr G. Coupe
Carnbargus Hartsbourne Mattie	B	19–5–70	Sh. Ch. Carnbargus Hartsbourne O'Brady	Sh. Ch. Hartsbourne Starlight	Mrs E. K. Walker	Mrs E. Gardner
Joanma's Kayla	B	3–4–69	Wendover Game	Joanma's Fora	Mrs E. A. Ward	Mrs T. Buffet
Joanma's Rachel	B	17–12–66	Joanma's Jimmy	Joanma's Cherie	Mrs M. J. Waters	Mrs M. Jarosz
Marrona Meriel	B	27–4–69	Sh. Ch. Scotswood Barabbas	Marrona Marstock Witch	Owner	Mrs M. E. Stokes
Moyna Michelle	B	29–9–71	Sh. Ch. Twoacres Troilus	Sh. Ch. Morningstar Melanie	Mrs B. Birch	Mrs S. P. Stobo
Wendover Happy-go-Lucky	B	26–4–70	Sh. Ch. Wendover Royalist	Ruani Redhead	Miss Besford	Mr and Mrs L. C. James
1975 Goldings Joss Cambier	D	2–4–71	Sh. Ch. Twoacres Troilus	Wendover Bonnie	Mr and Mrs G. Evans	Mrs Y. C. Edwards

Name	*Sex*	*Birth*	*Sire*	*Dam*	*Breeder*	*Owner*
Orichalc Alchymist	D	18–9–70	Sh. Ch. Cornevon Prince Charming	Orichalc Juneberry	Owner	Mrs V. J. Page
Wendover Jeeves	D	17–7–71	Sh. Ch. Wendover Ballymoss	Wendover Lupina	Owner	Mr and Mrs L. C. James
Wistavon Patrick	D	29–10–71	Highcray Swagman	Blairaven Cindy	Owner	Mr W. G. Staples
Caskeys Zoe	B	7–11–70	Caesars Fine Fella	Caskeys Cleoni	Owner	Mr and Mrs R. Heron
Cornevon Love Story	B	14–1–71	Sh. Ch. Cornevon Prince Charming	Sh. Ch. Cornevon Primrose	Mrs J. M. Roberts	Mr and Mrs B. Clarkson
Fearnley Fireflight	B	16–11–70	Sh. Ch. Wendover Racketeer	Fearnley Firefly	Owner	Mr and Mrs B. F. Rhodes
Ch. Laurie of Allsquare	B	28–6–70	Brackenfield Dandelion	Brackenfield Wistful	Mr J. M. Johnston	Mr J. Brown
Moval Bronze Model	B	13–3–72	Sh. Ch. Timadon Kendel	Moval Sowerhill Grand Sophy	Mrs M. Edwards	Mr and Mrs R. J. Cleland
1976 Ballywestow Kelso	D	15–2–71	Sh. Ch. Bidford Buffin	Ballywestow Frieze	Owner	Miss J. M. Russell
Cornevon Mercury	D	25–9–70	Sh. Ch. Cornevon Snowstorm	Sh. Ch. Cornevon Cinderella	Mrs J. M. Roberts	Mrs A. N. Trott
Cornevon Stargem	D	9–1–73	Sh. Ch. Twoacres Troilus	Sh. Ch. Cornevon Primrose	Mrs. J. M. Roberts	Mrs J. Harte

Moyna Mr O'Hara	D	4–7–70	Sh. Ch. Twoacres Troilus	Sh. Ch. Morningstar Melanie	Mrs B. Birch	Mr G. H. Perry
Raycroft Bosun	D	30–4–73	Sh. Ch. Corriecas Baron	Raycroft Tralee	Owner	Mrs C. E. Furness
Shanell Lerouge	D	21–10–71	Sh. Ch. Twoacres Troilus	Shama of Shanell	Mrs M. McCartney	Mrs C. Rose
Sowerhill Storm	D	13–1–74	Sh. Ch. Stephenshill Gamebird	Sh. Ch. Sowerhill Red Colleen of Kitewood	Miss O. M. Hunt	Mr J. Baglow
Wendover Marauder	D	14–4–71	Sh. Ch. Wendover Vagabond	Wendover Humorist	Mr and Mrs L. C. James	Mrs K. and Miss J. Norman
Ballywestow Keysoe	B	15–2–71	Sh. Ch. Bidford Buffin	Ballywestow Frieze	Owner	Miss J. M. Russell
Bella Rosa of Andana	B	7–10–71	Sh. Ch. Wendover Gentleman	Gay Serenade of Andana	Mrs H. B. Anderson	Mr and Mrs J. Rutherford
Cornevon Woodsprite	B	12–6–72	Sh. Ch. Cornevon Snowstorm	Sh. Ch. Cornevon Violet	Mrs J. M. Roberts	Miss J. E. Bacon
Emmafield Carefree	B	13–11–73	Sh. Ch. Orichalc Alchymist	Emmafield Beck	Owner	Mrs J. M. Aspinall
Gewdore Kala	B	20–9–72	Sh. Ch. Cornevon Lovebird	Linvid Gewdore Amber	R. K. Robertson	Miss Robertson
Joanma's Scampi	B	21–5–73	Sh. Ch. Joanma's Saffron	Joanma's Collette	Owner	Mrs M. Jarosz

Name	*Sex*	*Birth*	*Sire*	*Dam*	*Breeder*	*Owner*
1977 Gewdore Morello	B	1–12–73	Sh. Ch. Cornevon Lovebird	Linvid Gewdore Amber	R. K. Robertson	K. Wood
Meadway Bernice	B	27–7–69	Sh. Ch. Wendover Gentleman	Marchioness of Bickenhall	Mr & Mrs J. R. Edden	Miss K. Goodwin
Orichalc Quadrille	D	9–3–73	Sh. Ch. Orichalc Alchymist	Orichalc Illora	Mrs V. Page	A. D. Kelley
Ronetta Wild Rose of Kylende	B	5–8–72	Brenrue Benedictine of Brackenfield	Marie Rose of Ronetta	R. Cordwell	Mrs J. A. Morley
Scotswood Fara	B	16–6–72	Highcray Swagman	Scotswood Oola	Mrs W. Bryden	Mrs W. Bryden
Twoacres Wayward Caesar	D	31–11–72	Sh. Ch. Wendover Ballymoss	Musbury Melisande of Twoacres	Mrs J. Coates	Mr & Mrs G. Hogsflesh
Wendover Colas	D	1–9–72	Sh. Ch. Wendover Gentleman	Wendover Scarlet Girl of Kerrydene	Mr & Mrs L. C. James	Mr & Mrs B. A. Gurney
FT Ch. Whinbank Red Swallow	B	20–4–75	FT Ch. Grouse of Maytown	Loughharoon Red Tara	Owner	R. Law
FT Ch. Clashawley Gem	B	10–2–75	Moanruad Kerrygold	Moanruad Clareen	J. Ryan	Mrs J. Hague
1978 Joanma's Ranter	D	12–2–72	Sh. Ch. Joanma's Saffron	Sh. Ch. Joanma's Rachel	Mrs M. Jarosz	Mr J. Hickman
Allsquare Micky Finn	D	2–5–74	Sh. Ch. Cornevon Lovebird	Sh. Ch. Flame of Allsquare	Owner	Mr J. M. Johnston

Brandy Royale of Wendover	D	25–1–74	Sh. Ch. Wendover Racketeer	Wendover Hula Dancer	Mrs & Miss Norman	Mr & Mrs E. G. Durand
Wynjill Red Robin	D	29–8–73	Margretwoods Caretaker of Scotswood	Cornevon Tranquil	Owner	Mrs J. E. Holley
Ruani Kings Treasure	D	11–8–71	Ballywestow Dante	Ruani Redhead	Miss C. Besford	Mrs A. Allen
Tamarisk Tarragon of Duskhunter	B	24–3–72	Sh. Ch. Carnbargus Hartsbourne O'Brady	Tamarisk Bronze Bryony	Mrs S. Thomas	Miss L. Stewart
Chetruda Della of Coleraine	B	26–5–73	Sh. Ch. Shannel le Rouge	Sheena of Coleraine	Owner	Mrs V. Lockhart
Hartsbourne Periwinkle	B	17–3–74	Sh. Ch. Brackenfield Tertius	Hartsbourne Velvet	Owner	Miss S. J. Lennox
Heathcliffe Joanna	B	2–5–73	Hartsbourne Comet	Heathcliffe Hartsbourne Suzette	Owner	Miss B. Worth
Fearnley Firegem	B	17–5–76	Sh. Ch. Ruani Kings Treasure	Fearnley Fireopal	Mr & Mrs B. F. Rhodes	Mrs E. Rishworth
Cornevon Candida	B	21–8–73	Margretwoods Caretaker of Scotswood	Sh. Ch. Cornevon Cinderella	Owner	Mrs J. M. Roberts
1979 FT Ch. Franko of Crowhill	D	10–2–76	Knock Na Gaw	Moanruad Ragtime Skelan	Owner	P. Stewart
Carek Red Fashion	D	9–2–75	Sh. Ch. Timadon Kendel	Twoacres Andrea	Mrs Y. Horrocks	Mr & Mrs G. J. O. Davies

Name	*Sex*	*Birth*	*Sire*	*Dam*	*Breeder*	*Owner*
Zorosean Agvamarina	D	10–10–75	Cornevon Diamond	Zorosean Tricel	Mrs B. S. Lincoln	Mrs P. Cady
Emmafield Double Dutch	D	9–11–76	Sh. Ch. Cornevon Westerhuy's Dream	Sh. Ch. Emmafield Aubanjon Adventuress	Owner	Mrs J. M. Aspinall
Cornevon Westerhuy's Dream	D	17–7–75	Sh. Ch. Cornevon Prince Charming	Sh. Ch. Cornevon Primrose	Mrs J. M. Roberts	Mrs W. Duynkerke & Mrs J. M. Roberts
Brendower Bronze Champagne	D	12–7–76	Ultor of Orichalc	Brendower Berry Red	Owner	Mrs B. Howe
Brendower Brown Sugar	B	2–6–74	Sh. Ch. Hartsbourne Trident	Brendower Vickie	Owner	Mrs B. Howe
Scarletti Hot Chocolate	B	16–1–76	Sh. Ch. Cornevon Stargem	Margretwoods Conductress	Owner	Mrs. R. J. Pike
Pollyanna of Caskeys	B	2–3–75	Fearnley Firespark	Caskeys Tarontelle	Mrs Rolands	Mr & Mrs R. Heron
Wickenberry Baroness	B	23–7–76	Baron of Wendover	Sh. Ch. Twoacres Traviata	Owner	Mrs J. Quinn
Astley's Portia of Rua	B	7–9–75	Rua's Damian's Dandy Avanti	Saffron's Girl	Mrs M. Korbel	Miss C. M. Tuite & Mrs M. E. P. Tuite
Cornevon Westerhuy's Cloggy	B	23–5–75	Margretwoods Caretaker of Scotswood	Cornevon Stargazer	Mrs J. M. Roberts	Mrs W. Duynkerke & Mrs J. M. Roberts
Fearnley Fire-cinders of Dallowgill	B	7–10–77	Sh. Ch. Cornevon Westerhuy's Dream	Fearnley Firesprite	Mr & Mrs B. F. Rhodes	Mr & Mrs P. Jackson

1980 Jason of Andana of Clonageera	D	1–1–74	Margretwoods Caretaker of Scotswood	Tralee of Andana	Mrs J. Anderson	Mr & Mrs J. Rutherford
Brinara Inula	D	6–8–76	Cornevon Starspangle	Brenrue Moselle of Brinara	Mrs B. D. Berry	Breeder
Spruce of Andana	D	3–5–75	Wendover Grandee	Purple Clover of Andana	Mrs J. Anderson	Miss V. Thorne-Baker
Sowerhill Sahib	D	30–1–77	Sh. Ch. Wendover Jeeves	Sowerhill Sarah	Miss O. M. Hunt	Mrs S. Wood
Hartswelin Classy Catrina	B	28–3–77	Fearnley Firespark	Hartswelin Lovely Lady	Owners	Mesdames Coleman & Dormer
Wynjill Country Fragrance	B	7–3–75	Sh. Ch. Wynjill Red Robin	Sh. Ch. Cornevon Woodsprite	Owner	Mrs J. Holley
Berle of Brackenfield	B	18–4–74	Sh. Ch. Brackenfield Tertius	Hartsbourne Primrose	Mr J. Yool	Miss S. J. Lennox
Sowerhill Sarah	B	11–7–73	Sh. Ch. Stephenshill Gamebird	Sowerhill Samantha	Owner	Miss O. M. Hunt
Ballywestow Petite Etoile	B	7–3–78	Sh. Ch. Twoacres Wayward Caesar	Sh. Ch. Ballywestow Keysoe	Miss J. M. Russell	Mr & Mrs D. Williams
FT Ch. Glenside Red Hugh	D	30–1–73	Glenside Red	Churchfield Lady	Owner	P. J. McCabe
FT Ch. Hawk of Hogan's Wood	D	22–4–76	Moanruad Kerrygold	Moymore Colleen	M. Keniry	R. Law

BIBLIOGRAPHY

Baldwin, Dr T. A., 'Setters (Irish)' in the 1910 *Kennel Encyclopaedia*. Also published separately.

Baron, Bernard and Wilma, '1975 Official National Pictorial of the Irish Setter Club of America Inc.'

Barton, Frank Townend, *Gun Dogs*, 1913

Beazley, John M., Manners Alfred, K. and White-Robinson, Arnold C., *Training Pointers and Setters for Field Trials*, 1973.

Bepler, Mrs M. Ingle and Ryan, C. W., *Setters, Irish, English and Gordon*, second edition 1937.

Burns, Marca and Fraser, Margaret N., *Genetics of the Dog*. Second edition, 1966.

Carbery, J. A., 'The Irish Setter', *Hounds and Dogs*, 1932.

—'The Irish Setter', *Hutchinson's Dog Encyclopaedia*, vol. 2, 1934.

Cox, Major Harding, *Dogs and I*, 1923.

Compton, Herbert (editor), *The Twentieth Century Dog*, sporting volume, 1904.

Crew, F. A. E., *Animal Genetics*, 1925.

Dalziel, Hugh, *British Dogs*, vol. 1, 1879–80.

Day, J. Wentworth, *The Dog in Sport*, 1938.

Drury, W. D. (editor), *British Dogs*. Third edition, 1903.

Gray, Sir James, *How Animals Move*, 1953.

Hagedoorn, A. L. (revised by Allan Fraser), *Animal Breeding*, 1962.

Hutchinson, W. H., *Dog Breaking*. First edition 1848, Popular edition 1909.

Jacquet, E. W., *The Kennel Club, A History and Record of its Work*, 1905.

Kennel Club Stud Books, first annual volume published 1874.

Laverack, Edward, *The Setter*, 1872.

Lee, Rawdon B., *Modern Dogs*, Sporting division, first edition 1893, fourth edition 1914.

Leighton-Boyce, Gilbert, *Irish Setters*. Second impression, 1974.

Mason, Mrs A., 'The Irish Setter', *The Complete Book of Gundogs in Britain*, 1974.

Maurice, J. B., *Training Pointers and Setters*, 1974.

Millner, Col. J. K., *The Irish Setter. Its History and Training*, 1924.

Naylor, Leonard, *The Irish Setter: its history, temperament and training*, 1932.

Onstott, Kyle (revised by Philip Onstott), *The New Art of Breeding Better Dogs*, 1962.

Pearce, Rev. Thomas ('Idstone'), *The Dog*, 1872.

Redlick, Anna, *The Dogs of Ireland*, 1979.

Schilbred, Lt. Col. Corn, *Pointer og Setter*, Oslo, 1924. Irish Setter section, translated under the title of 'Irish Setter History', by William C. Thompson and O. Wallo, New York, 1949.

Scott, J. P. and Fuller, J. L., *Genetics and the Social Behaviour of the Dog*. The University of Chicago Press, 1965.

Slaughter, Frank, *The One Dog and the Others*, 1907.

Smythe, R. H., *The Conformation of the Dog*, 1957.

—*The Anatomy of Dog Breeding*, 1962.

Taylor, Ron and Renee, *The Irish Setter Club of America Pictorial*, 1970.

Teasdale-Buckell, G. T., *The Complete Shot*, 1907.

Thompson, William C., *The New Irish Setter*, New York 1967.

Trench, C. Chenevix, *The Shooter and His Gun*, 1969.

Walsh, J. H. ('Stonehenge'), *The Dogs of the British Islands*. Third edition, 1878.

—*The Dog in Health and Disease*, 1859.

Waters, B. (Kingrail), *Modern Training and Handling*. Third edition, Boston, 1905.

Watson, James, *The Dog Book*, vol. 1, 1906.

Whitney, Leon F., *How to Breed Dogs*. Third edition, New York, 1971.

Youatt, William, *The Dog*. First edition, 1845.

Index